PROFESSIONAL WRESTLING

PERFORMANCE STUDIES
Expressive Behavior in Culture

Sally Harrison-Pepper, General Editor

PROFESSIONAL WRESTLING

Sport and Spectacle

Sharon Mazer

UNIVERSITY PRESS OF MISSISSIPPI
Jackson

Photographs by Sharon Mazer unless otherwise noted.

Copyright © 1998 by University Press of Mississippi
All rights reserved
Manufactured in the United States of America
01 00 99 98   4 3 2 1

Library of Congress Cataloging-in-Publication Data

Mazer, Sharon.
    Professional wrestling : sport and spectacle / Sharon Mazer.
        p.   cm. — (Performance studies)
    Includes bibliographical references (p.   ) and index.
    ISBN 1-57806-020-6 (cloth : alk. paper). — ISBN 1-57806-021-4
(pbk. : alk. paper)
    1. Wrestling—Social aspects—United States.   2. Wrestling—United
States.   I. Title.   II. Series: Performance studies (Jackson,
Miss.)
GV1196.4.S63M39   1998
796.812'0973—dc21   97-42266
                                                 CIP

British Library Cataloging-in-Publication data available

Contents

Illustrations

Acknowledgments

More than seven years ago I took a much-needed break from my intensive reading in Middle English drama and, as was my custom, climbed on the exercycle in my kitchen, switched on the television, and began pedaling furiously. What I saw on the screen made me stop short and laugh. There was Ravishing Rick Rude entering to "The Stripper," insulting the men in the audience, dropping his sequined robe to reveal lycra trunks painted front and back with a cartoon image of the Ultimate Warrior, and cheating his way to a victory, which he then rudely celebrated by swiveling his hips over the Warrior's prone body and kissing a woman from the audience. The WWF broadcast that day immediately and irrevocably brought my readings in Middle English drama to life. Here was the play of vice and virtue, not as a historical remnant—a few texts of cycle, moral and saint plays, some town records, and a couple of illustrations—but as a part of my own theatrical and social present. In that moment I decided that I would find a way to write about professional wrestling. And while writing about wrestling has made my initial appreciation of its theatricality and values more complex and, I hope, more profound, I am grateful most of all for the pleasures of watching the sport and spectacle that is professional wrestling.

First I must thank the wrestlers themselves, especially Johnny Rodz, who first welcomed me into Gleason's Arena in 1989. Not only did he share his own stories and ideas about wrestling with me, he created an atmosphere in which the other wrestlers felt free to work in front of and talk with me. Of the many wrestlers who have spoken with me at length, I want to thank by name Larry, Chris, Vito, Rubio, Frankie, Sky, and

Mohammed. In addition, Steve Planamenta at the WWF provided me with important background information, as did Captain Lou Albano. Bil Mikulewicz shared his experiences as a designer for the WWF with me, while Henry Jenkins IV and Ben Lagerstrom were highly influential in my thinking about the place of the fans in the wrestling universe.

As this book has emerged, countless people—editors, colleagues, wrestlers, and friends—have shared their ideas and experiences in response to my work. In particular, I would like to thank Carol Martin for her thoughtful and precise reading of the manuscript at its most crucial moment and for insisting that I take the same care in my own thinking and writing. Larry DeGaris, who as Larry Brisco plays a central role in my stories of the wrestlers at Gleason's Gym, both responded to the writing and reminded me frequently and cheerfully that no matter how much I may come to understand the game I am still a mark, albeit a smart and perceptive mark, and as such still capable of being conned into believing what I see. Jessica Johnston and Vernon Andrews heroically read and commented on the first draft of the manuscript when the deadline for submission was fast approaching. Ongoing conversations with Peter Falkenberg and Bob Vorlicky have provoked much of my thinking about the performance of masculinity and violence, and many of their ideas have been integrated into my own. In addition, over the years Donna Heiland, John Bell, and Imogen de la Bere have supported my work with constant conversations, coffee, and good cheer. Henry Jenkins III and Chad Dell have shared their thinking and writing about professional wrestling with me, while my dissertation sponsor at Columbia University, Howard Schless, not only indulged my frequent digressions from Middle English drama into wrestling but shared with me his perspective as a former coach of high school wrestlers. JoAnne Prichard, the executive editor at the University Press of Mississippi, and Sally Harrison-Pepper, the series editor, have been supremely patient and supportive as I've worked my way through this project.

Although there was once a television program called *On the Mat* here, New Zealand currently has no professional wrestling culture of its own. But many of my students here and in New York still harbor vivid memories of matches and superstars, nonetheless, and some even admit to having been fanatic WWF fans when they were younger. I would like to thank the following students for providing me with a number of provocative conversations and essays on the topic, as well as encouragement, energy, and the occasional bouquet: Jenny Alexander, Greta Bond, Rosie Carnahan, Peter Currie, Michael Cusdin, Jane Ferrier, Olivia Harding, Chérie Hart, Kate McAnergney, Myfanwy Moore, and "the Ultimate" Jonno Roberts. In addition, my secretary, Jenner Lichtwark, stepped into the process at the last minute to help me select and organize the photographs as well as prepare the manuscript.

It was Richard Schechner who gave me a way of beginning. He pointed me toward Gleason's and then acted as a sharp and generous editor of my earliest drafts, teaching me heaps about research and writing in the process. For his encouragement then and in the years since, I would like to thank him once again.

Finally, I must offer my deepest gratitude to my husband, Gary Carsel, and to our daughter, Casey Larkin, for gracefully accepting my absence over the summer holiday in New Zealand so that I could write full-time. Gary has always taken my writing about professional wrestling seriously, even when I haven't, and it is to him that this book is dedicated.

PROFESSIONAL WRESTLING

Chapter One

"REAL" WRESTLING

Hey Professor, lemme tell you a story.
          —The Wildman Dave McKigney

I thought we were on the inside together.
          —Clifton Jolley

"Why don't you take pictures of us naked? Huh? Huh? You want pictures? Take pictures of us naked!" Vito, a large wrestler with a shaved head who sometimes appears as "Von Kraut" for the World Wrestling Federation (WWF), is shouting, menacing me as I circle the ring at Gleason's Gym with my camera (20 February 1993). The other wrestlers watch and listen, but otherwise leave us alone. Taken aback, I reply: "Why would I want to do that? I'm an academic." It's a lame response, I realize immediately. But nothing more effective springs to mind. Instead, I remember the incident on ABC-TV's *20/20* when reporter John Stossel had his ears boxed by David Schultz after insisting that the monster wrestler admit that professional wrestling is not "real" wrestling. Instead of coming up with a pithy response, I realize once more that I don't belong in a steamy gym watching a bunch of men practice hitting each other, or pretending to hit each other. I belong in a library, at a computer, at a coffee bar with a friend discussing Foucault. . . . I remember that Vito is a big man who could inflict considerable injury if he stops shouting at me and decides to act. I remember that he is a man and I am a woman, and that there are tensions, created by the mere fact of my presence in the gym, that could explode at me if I am not careful.

But Vito doesn't do more than repeat his challenge, which I continue to parry without much success. The exchange goes on for what seems like an hour until he at last stalks off to the locker room. When Vito reemerges and joins the other men hanging around the ring, Johnny—as in "the Unpredictable Johnny Rodz School of Professional Wrestling"—jokes that we should do a series of photos in which I'm wrestling the men to the mat and then casually offers me a ride back into Manhattan, an escape I gratefully accept. Upon my rather cautious return to the gym the following Saturday, Vito ignores me for an hour or so and then approaches me. I try to contain my anxiety, but instead of attacking me once more, he earnestly asks me about his chances of breaking into the film business as an actor, and we resume our customary, if sometimes wary, dialogue.

What happened? What was I—a member of the cultural elite—doing on the receiving end of a wrestler's tirade? For that matter, what was I—short, round, and female, not inclined to athletics of any sort—doing sitting on a metal chair ringside watching a group of men working out on yet another Saturday afternoon?

It's been many years since I first found my way to the Unpredictable School of Professional Wrestling. I've spent months at a stretch watching wrestlers train, taking notes and photographs first for an article published in the *Drama Review* in 1990 and subsequently as part of ongoing research for a series of conference papers and now this book.[1] Because Johnny accepts me, the younger wrestlers have, for the most part, tolerated my presence, ignoring or welcoming me according to their individual, moment-to-moment inclinations. The confrontation with Vito was an exception, a vivid reminder that no matter how much time I spend ringside at Gleason's, I don't really belong. Trained as I have been in the theatre and in the academy, not in the ring, I have been forced to acknowledge that I am a scholar, not a wrestler, that while I may watch wrestling, what I write is, in the end, about performance.

Professional wrestling is integral to and representative of American culture on multiple levels. Sometimes referred to as "sports entertainment"—the term was coined in the 1980s as part of WWF promoter Vince McMahon's effort to get licensing restrictions eased—professional wrestling is a sport that is not, in the literal sense of the word, sporting; a theatrical entertainment that is not theatre. Its display of violence is less a contest than a ritualized encounter between opponents, replayed repeatedly over time for an exceptionally engaged audience. The colorful characters presented and the stories told both in the wrestling ring and in the television programming that contextualizes matches are simultaneously archetypal and topical, open to straightforward readings but in that very openness resistant to simple readings of dominant cultural values. Although it is most often compared by scholars to the medieval moral play, or psychomachia, as in Middle English drama professional wrestling's presentations of virtue and vice are more ambiguous than might be apparent at first glance, the event more carnival than Mass. Rather than simply reflecting and reinforcing moral clichés, professional wrestling puts contradictory ideas into play, as with its audience it replays, reconfigures, and celebrates a range of performative possibilities.

To watch wrestling and then to write about performance is to attempt to confront and come to terms with the significance of a highly popular performance practice as it intersects, exploits, and finally parodies the conventions of both sport and theatre. Professional wrestling attracts and sustains extraordinarily large audiences. In local communities these audiences number in the hundreds or even thousands for live events and in the thousands for regional broadcasts via cable television. In the big leagues, nationally and internationally, the numbers begin in the tens of thousands at live events and can run into the millions with televised broadcasts and video sales. The sheer numbers of performers and spectators certainly indicate a mass cultural appeal. The numbers also point toward a heterogeneity that contradicts conventional assumptions about professional wrestling's low- and working-class audiences.

This study remains focused on the American version of professional wrestling, a form that, while still connected to the origins of wrestling in the ancient world, emerged in the carnivals and fairgrounds of the nineteenth century and developed along with television from the middle of the twentieth century to the present day. At the same time, it is important to remember that a large number of countries have their own professional wrestling traditions that interact with the American, but are specific to their own historical and contemporary contexts. In addition, Japanese and Mexican (known as Lucha Libre) wrestlers and promotions are popular in the United States, and American wrestlers often appear in promotions in these countries as well as in other parts of the world.

As the one sport in which participants lose legitimacy when they move from "amateur" to "professional," professional wrestling is actually a genre of sports spectacle, defined by its style rather than by the fact that its participants are paid for their performances. Professional wrestling, with its fast and high-flying acrobatics, glitzy costumes, and hot talk, works and looks quite different from amateur wrestling. Beyond the spectacular elements, many of which are now common in many other sports as well, professional wrestling is an athletic performance practice that is constructed around the display of the male body and a tradition of cooperative rather than competitive exchanges of apparent power between men. Professional wrestlers learn the rules of the game as athletic skills, as performance practice, and as masculine ethos. Through a kinetic process of observation, repetition, demonstration, and correction in interaction with other wrestlers, they imprint the moves in their bodies: lifts and slams, holds and reversals. At the same time they learn to strategize their performances: how to take hits as well as dish them out, when to back off and when to press forward, what to show an audience and what to conceal, how to engage their audiences in an active call and response, and how to combine the moves into sequences in the moment-to-moment improvisation of the performance within the parameters of traditional and/or fixed scenarios as a way of making their performances both logical and appealing to audiences. Above all, professional wrestlers learn to create their performances in collusion with each other implicitly and with the audience explicitly. To learn the rules of the game means to learn to give respect as well as demand it, to put the other guy over as well as to generate heat for oneself, to be a man who displays loss and pain as well as one who celebrates his apparent dominance over this week's loser.

Professional wrestling explicitly and implicitly makes visible cultural and countercultural ideas of masculinity and sexuality. Wrestling's apparently conservative masculine ideal is constantly undermined through the parodic, carnivalesque presentation of its opposite. Professional wrestling's often vehement heterosexism is thus underscored by the homoerotic. What men do in the ring is to touch each other in ways that are only superficially violent. On the surface, what is performed, what an audience sees, is a range of masculine identities in which the virtuous man can be recognized by the way in which he plays by the rules and courts the audience's approval, and victory always equals masculinity. By definition, it is always the best man who wins. But in the structured give and take of the match, every man gets a chance to demonstrate his potential for victory. Even Gorgeous George regularly dropped his drag in the middle of a match to exhibit his power and skill in dominating his opponent, though he then stopped to pat his hair back into place.

Indeed, when it comes to the representation of gender, the underlying discourse of the professional wrestling event is essentially essentialist. While women who perform as wrestlers and managers train and perform much as the men do, the presence of women in the wrestling performance is substantially different. Male wrestlers may be seen to reveal, in the display of their bodies and in their actions, their real manliness. Conversely, what women reveal in their bodily displays and performances is that no matter how closely their actions converge on those of men, they are not and can never be men. And as they mark the place of the not-at-all-manly man, their displays almost inevitably verge explicitly on the pornographic. As such, although women are visibly involved at all levels—as wrestlers, promoters, managers, and spectators—professional wrestling is a male-centered performance practice. Whatever else is performed, what is presented, affirmed, and critiqued is nothing so much as the idea(l) of masculinity itself. As such, the question of what it means to be a man in contemporary culture underlies the continuous display of manly and not-so-manly behavior in and out of the ring. It might be easy to read wrestling's representations of masculinity as in keeping with assumptions of (lower) cultural clichés: the manly man is the good guy who eschews feathers and sequins, keeps his gimmicks to a minimum, and is virtuous in the struggle against the bad guy; the bad guy precisely opposes and acts against these values. But in the conventionalized give and take of the ring, what is revealed in even the most flamboyantly feminine male wrestler's performance is his essential masculinity. As it displays, parodies, and mocks masculinity, professional wrestling may be seen to celebrate a range of masculinities in which the only not-real man is a woman, and even that may not always be certain.

Professional wrestling is often seen as a suspect sport and a marginal entertainment. Beyond the question of the "fix"—and that finishes are most often fixed is not in question here—professional wrestling appears to violate basic principles of masculine performance in a number of ways. First, it relies on the display of male bodies that are presented alternately in extravagant costumes and almost naked. Second, these male bodies in performance are seen to touch and embrace, to make a show but not a reality of hurting another man, to dominate and submit to one another in ways that resemble nothing so much as clichés of sexual engagement. Fiercely heterosexual and heterosexist in its discourse, professional wrestling thus converges on the homoerotic in its semiotics. On the surface, professional wrestling may be profoundly conservative, representing truth, justice, and the dream of the ideal American man. At the same time, however, it is highly transgressive, offering its spectators ways of reading and engaging that extend well beyond the surface.

Wrestling, then, is a hybrid performance practice: a professional sport in which players can earn their livings at the same time that it offers its audiences a spectacle that goes beyond contest into theatrical spectacle. In this light it is important to ask what makes wrestling so popular in contemporary culture, to see what it is the fans actually see in the arenas, big and small, as well as on television. That is, it is important to examine both the surface of the performance and the way in which it is constructed, to interrogate the promoter's promise to give fans their money's worth and the fans' demand that that promise be kept, and to consider the display of violence between men as a macrocosmic expression of masculine identities and cultural conflicts.

Because the promoters and performers are explicit in their salesmanship, because the performance caters directly to the fans, and because the game is structured around their active participation *as* fans, the spectators are always visible and, at least superficially, empowered in the wrestling event. Far from being a secret or a problem for wrestling fans, the fact that finishes of most professional wrestling matches are fixed is part of what pulls them to the arenas and their televisions again and again. Professional wrestling fans are always in a process of becoming insiders. They are self-conscious about coming to see what they see and to know what they know, which is always more than they saw or knew in the past. They don't so much suspend disbelief as they sustain it while looking for moments in which to believe. They look to see the fake and to see through the fake to the real. They scrutinize performances, examining each punch for its impact or nonimpact and matches for the logic of the exchanges as they evaluate the story lines and angles offered on the basis of believability in relation to the "real" world. The pleasure peculiar to wrestling is in the way in which it engages its audiences directly in its play, in affirming and challenging cultural norms, and in believing and disbelieving in what it sees at the same time.

Extant scholarly writing on wrestling may be seen to swing between the personal and the more objective. What a survey of the literature ultimately reveals is the range of theoretical discourses that may be applied to wrestling. What seems inescapable—regardless of the proximity or distance of the writer and regardless of theoretical orientation—is that professional wrestling is recognized and ultimately serves as a metaphor for social structures and meanings. The squared circle, like the medieval stage, comes to represent the world itself. Its oppositions, hierarchies, conventions, and transgressions become at once more and less than what might actually be perceived in the ring itself. Like the fans, scholars must learn to balance the seen against the unseen when watching wrestling, to perceive and sustain the contradictions as part of a performance practice that is more complicated than it at first appears.

Many studies find it convenient to reinscribe the dramaturgical conventions of professional wrestling into theatrical or folkloric models, often eliding the distinction between sport and theatre or sport and ritual in order both to make their points and to recuperate wrestling from its status as a less than legitimate form. Moreover, most are reliant on assumptions of the wrestling fans' lower-class naïveté and working-class anger for their rationalizations of wrestling's moral and social messages. As a consequence, academic studies of professional wrestling are best defined by the writers' relative proximity to the ring. While Jim Freedman announces himself as an academic, he almost immediately enters into the wrestling world as an active participant, so that the narrative he produces in *Drawing Heat* is almost entirely personal as he describes his journey from his first awkward venture into the offices of the promoters to his travels with the Wildman Dave McKigney and the wrestling bear. At the other extreme, in *Wrestling to Rasslin: Ancient Sport to American Spectacle*, Gerald W. Morton and George M. O'Brien construct their account of professional wrestling's historical development and ritual aspects as spectators, and even then at a distance that is often almost completely removed from the arena. Most engaging are the enthusiasms of noted writers Roland Barthes (in "The World of Wrestling") and Angela Carter (in "Giants' Playtime") as they wax lyrical about professional wrestling's spectacular semiotics. But in such eloquence the wrestling event becomes more myth than actuality. Overall, most studies focus on professional wrestling as a theatrical event or as a contemporary example of folk culture.[2] What they have in common is their presentation of wrestling's underlying social and moral ethos as a model of lower-class expressions of the desire for a nonambiguous moral order where virtue may not always prevail, but it is easily recognizable and always worth cheering.[3]

It is the question of the "fake" that dominates most casual and scholarly discussions of professional wrestling. How can professional wrestling be "real" wrestling if the outcomes of contests are fixed, the winners and the way of winning determined by the promoters in advance? How can professional wrestling be taken seriously as a sport, let alone discussed in a scholarly context, when the men and women who participate at every level—wrestlers, managers, promoters, even fans—must all be seen to be pretending at best, lying and perpetrating a con at worst? Certainly nobody with any sense over the age of, say, eleven believes that these men are really hurting each other! But professional wrestlers, promoters, managers, and fans are absolutely serious, insistent that the game be played according to the rules. Yes, the finishes are fixed—that's not in question—and scenarios are frequently discussed, if not actually rehearsed, in advance. But what is at stake is not winning or losing per se. Rather it is, literally, the way in which the game is played. In that professional wrestlers play the game according to the protocols both of the sport and of masculinity, professional wrestling more than any other sport may be seen to fulfill the clichés of sportsmanlike conduct. Most important, the fact of the fix itself fixes professional wrestling as a macrocosmic expression of a worldview in which the struggle for success whether in the ring or in life is never really a fair fight.

To watch wrestling over time, to become a fan and a borderline participant in the culture of the ring, is to come to recognize the ways in which its apparent simplicities of characterization and narrative contain, sustain, and ultimately celebrate contradictory social and moral messages. I have sat with the fans, cheering and jeering the action, snapping pictures and keeping up with the commentary both from the ring and in the stands for WWF events at Madison Square Garden and for Johnny's school shows at Gleason's Arena in Brooklyn. One time, memorably, I even took the "wrestling bus" from New York City to the Meadowlands Arena in New Jersey where diversity of wrestling fans was perhaps most vivid. Among the twenty thousand or so spectators who surrounded my husband and me were a pair of women who looked like retired school-teachers (one black and one white) and who yelled and carried on with tremendous glee; a middle-class black family with children running up and down the steps to get a closer look and to cheer their favorites; a white male homosexual couple who were relatively quiet and inner-directed; an elderly black man in an ancient fedora who held his program like a race card; a group of Asian yuppies who were as exuberant in their photo-taking as in their yells; and a man who looked like a James Dean impersonator in black T-shirt and jeans, with greased-back hair and a blond wife and children, whom he ignored as he narrated and predicted the entire performance for my husband's benefit. In addition to my grow-ing collection of Hulk Hogan dolls—all gifts from amused friends and family—I have collected numerous souvenir programs and fanzines, and I still keep up with the rec.sport.pro-wrestling (RSPW) discussion on the Internet, when time permits. With Henry Jenkins IV, a younger fan who has been avid about wrestling for some years, as a guide, I have even ventured into "virtual wrestling" for a few months; there I briefly held a tag-team title as "the Professor," whom I characterized as a cliché of the ninety-eight-pound weakling with the advantage of being managed by "the Librarian," a monster with a lethal bookbag.

All this is by way of saying that it's been tremendous fun, not at all like the pleasures peculiar to library and archival research. Moreover I have come to see that my own writing has been inflected by, if not in-fected with, the hyperbole that is at the heart of the wrestling experience. As someone who has spent an inordinate amount of time ringside, I admit that I have also acquired a certain sense of loyalty to the game and to the wrestlers and fans who have shared a part of their lives with me. At the same time, if I am to tell the truth about what happens now that I am no longer watching but writing, I have to acknowledge that these wrestlers and fans have become less themselves than characters in a nar-rative that I am constructing in service of my own ongoing examination of the relation between performance and culture. Because the materials available to me are endless—videotapes, magazines, newsletters, Internet discussions—and because live as well as televised professional wrestling performances are available to almost anyone who reads this, I have chosen a limited number of examples to which I return as paradigmatic of the larger world of wrestling. I have also bypassed a number of issues that seemed beyond the scope of this study. In particular, I have avoided the superficially simple but actually complex and often contradictory representations of race and nationality, in which the stereotypes—from homeboy to jailbreaker, from illegal immigrant to macho lover—in practice are largely absorbed both in wrestling's overriding need to present shifts of status between hero and villain and in its masculinist dramaturgy.[4] Above all, wherever possible I have tried to let the wrestlers, fans, and other participants speak for themselves as they once spoke to and around me.

At the heart of this analysis are my own experiences and observations of the training process at "the Unpredictable School of Professional Wrestling" in Brooklyn, New York. As new wrestlers are put through their paces and instructed in the rules of the game by more experienced wrestlers, the three levels on which learning happens come into focus: athletic, performative, and cultural. They learn how to do the moves by doing them repeatedly, endlessly. At the same time, they absorb lessons in presenting those moves to audiences, in creating a spectacle of violence that is not actually violent. The professional wrestler learns to "work": to contain his propensity for actual violence and to restrain his desire for dominance in order to make his performance of violence accessible to and engaging for an audience.

Watching wrestlers perform in the arena is relatively easy. One just has to purchase a ticket and remember who to cheer and who to jeer. Watching wrestlers work out in the gym requires, among other things, a certain tact. To win the wrestlers' acceptance—not just permission to sit ringside, but to hear the stories, to be allowed to take photographs, and ultimately to be "let in on the game"—has obliged me to accept a kind of dynamic invisibility. I have been silent for long hours and then, suddenly, asked to perform more actively as a kind of model spectator: "Ask Sharon. She knows," Johnny will goad a youngster. "Sure!" I chirp. Or, on stopping two wrestlers who are more inclined to fight each other in earnest, he will reiterate that it's not enough to do the moves and will remind them that "before you hit the guy you have to ask the audience, 'What should I do?' " When he turns to me, I contribute as cued: "Kill him!"

The wrestlers, following Johnny's example, have created their own ways of incorporating me into their domain, of converting my watch-ing—my intrusion into their private practice—into something less dis-turbing. Often a wrestler first begins to engage me in dialogue by inviting me to wrestle with him. The offer to teach me the moves is half jest, half test. What is at stake is not so much whether or not I'm going to get into the ring. I won't. The question is more how will I respond. Will I attempt to lecture them on what is theirs, patronize them? Will I be offended at the implication that I might come to their level, become touchable? I laugh because it's silly to expect me to last more than a fleeting second in the ring, despite their assurances that they'll only play with me. The wrestler generally laughs with me and on subsequent afternoons will find other ways of acknowledging me at least once or twice, if not approach-ing me for a full conversation. Often the last wrestler to jest/test me will tease a newcomer by introducing me as his "teacher" who has taught him everything he knows about the game. Inevitably, within about a month of encountering me for the first time, a wrestler will sidle up to me at ringside and interrogate me, as Vito once did: "So, you're writing a book, huh? You have a husband? What does he think of you hanging out at the gym with a bunch of wrestlers?"

My role as an observer has thus evolved via a series of interactions directed by Johnny and negotiated with the wrestlers on a day-to-day basis. Over the years I have come to realize just how problematic our transactions are. In that I have been permitted to show up at the gym, uninvited and unannounced, week after week, allowed to watch while refusing to enter the ring myself, I have been a voyeur. That is, I have been privileged as an audience of one to observe a group of men engaged in secret, essentially intimate exchanges. Watching wrestlers in their pri-vate training sessions is not exactly the same activity as being a spectator at a striptease or a Times Square peep show, but what I have done, liter-ally, is spend hours in close proximity to men in various stages of undress as they toss and hold each other, sharing secrets and experiences that ordinarily would exclude me completely.

The way in which the wrestlers monitor and judge my behavior ap-pears to be attached to, and reflective of, my status as a woman in an arena defined and dominated by men. As a scholar doing research, I am potentially a threat to the culture of the ring, to the way in which these men construct their relations to each other, and to their ambitions in the highly competitive industry that is professional wrestling, already problematized as the least legitimate of sports. I represent what they perceive as a dominant culture that effectively excludes and marginalizes them as lower-class men: "We've had people like you here before, come in here, think they can tell us what we're about," Larry Brisco said to me, early on. At the same time, as a woman in a predominantly male culture, I am both a threat and, superficially at least, familiar, proximate to their everyday experiences and expectations. My acceptance in the gym has, as a result, been contingent upon my own performance within conventional assumptions of femininity. To remain silent and effectively invisible while present, to speak only when spoken to and even then only according to the cues given, has signaled to these men my willingness to perform according to their (generally unspoken) rules. Because I have been what they might term "respectful"—or perhaps more properly, because I have not been disrespectful—I have been told by Johnny that I "don't have to get [my] face pushed to the mat to be let in on the game." Or haven't I?

Getting your face pushed to the mat is the rite of passage any newcomer to wrestling faces in the early weeks. Typically he unintentionally provokes the wrath of a more experienced wrestler who then verbally and physically abuses him as the others stand back and watch. If the newcomer sticks it out and returns subsequently, he has passed a crucial test, is deemed worthy of a higher degree of respect than before, and is assimilated into the group. It is indeed possible that Johnny's statement was not so much a compliment as an acknowledgment that my physicality makes me an obviously unsuitable candidate for rigorous athletic training. It may also be my short, round femaleness that softens any threat implicit in my watching. But it is clear that Vito's verbal assault—which felt no less frightening and humiliating for being in words rather than in punches—served as an equivalent initiation, a test of my willingness to stand my ground, to stick it out, and to return the next week for more if necessary.

Given that I was conscious of and playing by the rules, that I was being a good girl, why was Vito shouting at me? The short answer is that I spoke out of turn. Or rather, I spoke properly in response to a prompt from Johnny but failed to take into account the volatility of the particular wrestler. In brief, Johnny had stopped Vito as he was about to pummel his partner and asked him what he thought the (imagined) spectators' response would be to his failure to invite their participation. This is a standard exchange in Johnny's pedagogic repertoire, a lesson in engaging the audience in the action with which I was, by then, quite familiar. He turned to me, as he has on many occasions, and I chimed in with the expected spectator response: "Bor-ring!" At which point, the shouting began.

While it is true that I had acted according to the role assigned to me by Johnny, my shift from silent watcher to jeering spectator, however appropriate and even playful, at that moment transformed Vito's private lesson into a public humiliation, his workout with the other men into a display in front of a woman. His demand that I take pictures of them naked was, at this level, a direct response to his coming to awareness of being watched. His sense of having been exposed was to be matched by my own, his loss of face redeemed by mine. In his assault I was to be denied the safety of the sidelines. My invisibility was revoked. Given that I had spoken, the last word was to be his.

But of course the last word is literally mine. After Johnny dropped me off in Greenwich Village, I found a quiet café and, as was my habit, recorded the events of the day in my notebook. More than a year later I wrote the first draft of the essay in which this chapter now, another year later, finds its origins. In addition to joining the fans in the arena, watching matches on television, and reading the myriad fanzines, newsletters, and Internet discussions, I have been privileged to sit ringside first at Gleason's Arena and then at Gleason's Gym, to watch wrestlers without entering the ring myself, to share experiences that ranged from exhilarating to humiliating, to come to a place in the end that was not fully outside, not fully inside, but somehow balanced on the boundary between. As a result, this account is simultaneously personal and scholarly, as much the story of the distances I have traveled since beginning this research as it is about what I have seen wrestlers do, what I have heard them say, and what I think it means.

Chapter Two

WHAT THE *WORLD* IS WATCHING

> We are therefore dealing with a real Human Comedy, where
> the most socially-inspired nuances of passion (conceit,
> rightfulness, refined cruelty, a sense of "paying one's
> debts") always felicitously find the clearest sign which can
> receive them, express them and triumphantly carry them to
> the confines of the hall.
>
> —Roland Barthes

> This is Theatre of Cruelty played for laughs, in which in-
> jury is a regrettable accident. . . . A game with all the appear-
> ance of merciless combat, and all the trimmings of diverting
> make-believe.
>
> —Angela Carter

> Where the Big Boys Play.
>
> —WCW slogan

On Sunday, 2 April 1989, Macho Man Randy Savage battled to defend his World Wrestling Federation (WWF) national championship belt against challenger, former friend, and sometime tag-team
partner, Hulk Hogan in a spectacular showdown at *WrestleMania V*. For
a long time Hogan's demise seemed certain as we watched him, apparently to the end of his endurance, his forehead bleeding, struggle simply
to stay in the ring. But in the Main Event's final seconds, the "Hulkster"
(as he is known to his fans) miraculously recovered both his spirit and
his strength, turning the match around to wrench the title from his opponent. The audience at the Beacon Theatre in New York City, where we
watched the match as it was broadcast live from Atlantic City onto a
huge screen, was ecstatic at the dramatic reversal. They danced in the
aisles, mimicking Hogan's victory poses, shouting at and snapping pictures of the hero. After months of following the televised challenges, of

listening to the accusations and counteraccusations hurled between the two men, the American public was more than ready to see "The Mega-Powers Explode!"

WrestleMania V drew its enormous live audience through a variety of media. While nearly 20,000 people were present in the arena at the Trump Plaza in Atlantic City, approximately 100 audiences of 2,000 to 14,000 people each watched the event in closed-circuit auditoriums. In addition, another 915,000 households across the United States bought the pay-per-view broadcast. The *WrestleMania V* video was marketed to approximately 40 countries, with a pre-event sale of more than 120,000 copies.[1] By whipping such a large audience into a frenzy of anticipation and then delivering almost four hours of live entertainment climaxed by such a dramatic finale, the WWF had indeed earned the right to boast that it was "what the world is watching."

But *WrestleMania V* was only one event in a year-round display that annually engages phenomenal numbers of spectators. When I began this research in 1989, professional wrestling was undergoing one of its periodic peaks in visibility and popularity, largely as a result of the way in which WWF owner/promoter Vince McMahon had transformed the WWF's television presence, taking advantage of new technologies and techniques both in camera-work and in presentation. At that time, the WWF maintained a stable of 75 to 80 wrestlers who performed in more than 1,000 live events per year—events that, according to WWF media coordinator Steve Planamenta, drew 8 million spectators in 1987. Planamenta told me that an additional 20 million spectators were estimated to be tuning in weekly to the WWF's syndicated programs: *Superstars of Wrestling* and *Wrestling Challenge*. Professional wrestling, even more than other "professional" sports, is big business, not solely in its presentations of live performances around the world, but just as important in its ancillary marketing practices. Planamenta stated that the WWF takes in $200 million per year in merchandising alone. Their gate in 1988 was approximately $80 million. *WrestleMania V* alone took in $1.7 million. Add to these numbers the advertising revenues from the various prime-time and late-night specials, as well as income from cable programming and video sales around the world, and the WWF boast seems even more apt.

The WWF is by no means the only game in town. There are a multitude of local and regional circuits, each with its own set of initials: ECW, NCW, ICW, NWA, AWA, UWS, GLOW, POWW, to name just a few.

Most of the circuits have clearly delineated territories, both on the ground and on television (primarily cable and video). Most are local or regional concerns, with audiences that are loyal to local stars while also keeping up with the big league action via the television shows and live tours. The turf that WWF dominated in the 1980s and early 1990s is now fiercely contested by the WCW (World Championship Wrestling). Formerly the NWA (National Wrestling Alliance), the WCW was purchased by Ted Turner in 1989; Turner has reportedly paid tremendous sums of money to lure superstars—everyone from star wrestlers Hulk Hogan and Randy Savage to star commentators Mean Gene Okerlund and Bobby "the Brain" Heenan—away from the WWF. Indeed, the most recent *WrestleMania*, number twelve, featured a parody match between the "Huckster" and the "Nacho Man" as part of the ongoing war between the two circuits. The cost of active competition from the deep pockets of the Turner Broadcasting System to the WWF is reportedly quite high, leading Vince McMahon to protest publicly. But it also seems to have added a layer of appreciation for many of the hard-core fans, who now enthusiastically debate both the quality and the ratings of the two monster promotions.

Just what sort of performance is this that so many people are so eager to see? At its most elemental, professional wrestling is simply two men (or, much less frequently, women) engaged in a spectacle of violent conflict. Yet the professional event is resonant with a diverse range of performance and even nonperformance practices. In Angela Carter's words: "Sometimes professional wrestling is like chess, and sometimes like ballet, and sometimes like a crude morality play. . . . Sometimes it's like folk drama masquerading as sport; occasionally vaudeville. . . . Or else it is physical display decked out with certain elements of antique theatre, masks, hieratic posturing, menace, dread, violence, pain—all the apparatus of the Theatre of Cruelty, except its metaphysics" (227).

As in chess, pro wrestling's moves are conventionally circumscribed, its sequences shaped both by a kind of physics and by a macrocosmic understanding of character and logic: the white against the black, this is the way kings move, this the way pawns move. As in ballet, the performance is largely pantomimic, relying on the spectators' knowledge of its kinetic vocabulary; in wrestling as in dance, the wrestlers learn to place their bodies both in motion and at rest in much the same way as dancers learn the fundamentals of ballet. And even more than as in dance, as in contact improvisation, their movements are always in direct relation to one another, elaborated upon from one point of contact to the next. As with the Middle English morality play, the wrestling platform—the "squared circle" as it is commonly called—is a macrocosm of the world, the players representative of virtue and vice, and the struggle between them staged on terms that are eternal as well as temporal.[2] As in ancient tragedy, the spectator is engaged in something more than "the spectacle of a virtuous man brought from prosperity" or "that of a bad man passing from adversity to prosperity" (*Poetics* 75). In the words of Roland Barthes: "What is thus displayed for the public is the great spectacle of Suffering, Defeat, and Justice. Wrestling presents man's suffering with all the amplification of tragic masks" (19).

Hyperbole aside, Carter's recognition that professional wrestling works much as Artaud's Theatre of Cruelty, albeit evacuated of his metaphysical ambitions, is particularly astute. With its roots in the ancient and medieval worlds, with its hypersized displays of character and action, with its play at the edge of violence, professional wrestling reaches past the conscious responses of the spectators into the reflexive and visceral. In the ecstatic interactions of fans with each other and with performers in the arenas it is indeed possible to perceive an echo at least of the kind of "mass spectacle" that Artaud when conceptualizing the Theatre of Cruelty idealized as "the agitation of tremendous masses, convulsed and hurled against each other" (85). In this light, professional wrestling resembles the Balinese cockfight as described by Clifford Geertz, albeit without the actual death of the participants, when he tells us: "In the cockfight, man and beast, good and evil, ego and id, the creative power of aroused masculinity and the destructive power of loosened animality fuse in a bloody drama of hatred, cruelty, violence, and death" (420–21).

More commonly, Carter's idea of wrestling as a kind of folk drama is a comparison that is certainly echoed by most writers about wrestling. For all the big business done by the WWF and the WCW, professional wrestling events are still frequently staged in fairgrounds, carnivals, and school gymnasiums, as such a local affair, performed by and in the context of its own communities throughout the United States and, indeed, the world. In this light, Carter's aside about vaudeville is most apt in that, like vaudeville, wrestling is simultaneously a traditional performance with conventions by which characters and actions are presented and a topical performance, immediately responsive to current events and always reflective of the here and now.

What is revealed in the range of comparisons to other performance practices is wrestling's essential openness to reading and rereading from any number of positions for any number of purposes. Henry Jenkins calls wrestling a "masculine melodrama" and sees in it a reworking of the conventions of nineteenth-century melodrama and twentieth-century soap opera, in which the presentation of multiple characters in intersecting narratives, serialized performances of betrayal and revenge, and climactic displays of sufferings reflect the preoccupations of a predominantly male working- and lower-class audience. He notes that wrestling as "masculine melodrama confronts the painful paradox that working class men are powerful by virtue of their gender and vulnerable by virtue of their economic status" (44). Similarly, after reciting professional wrestling's antecedents in the ancient and medieval worlds, Morton and O'Brien are primarily concerned with wrestling as morality play and folk ritual, designed to enact the conflicts and expiate the anxieties and angers of its predominantly male working- and lower-class audience.[3] For my part, the professional wrestling event seems most accessible when considered in relation to both the morality play and the feast of fools. Its exchanges and oppositions—between speaking and acting, narrative and pantomime, virtue and vice, the ideal and the real, the manly and the not-so-manly, the "real" and the "fake"—are simultaneously abstract and concrete, stable and subject to radical transgression and even revisioning at any moment.

The professional wrestling performance combines breathtaking athleticism and prodigious showmanship. The wrestlers present themselves as larger-than-life figures from a comic-book-like world. They wear costumes that range from brief to extravagant, make their entrances to personalized theme music, carry trademark props, and offer signature gestures and shouts that spectators enthusiastically parrot back to the ring. Stories are developed over a series of confrontations between wrestlers, and spoken challenges, either in the ring or via television, repeatedly communicate the histories of the combatants and legitimize or delegitimize one wrestler's grudge against another, so that the context for a fight is immediately perceptible to the most neophyte spectator. The actual display of violence is a culmination of past confrontations and part of an accumulating series of encounters, centered on the shifting of power and allegiance between men. A fight is rarely finished at the bell. One thing always leads to another. As one match ends, the stage is invariably set for a return encounter. And always the wrestlers work to sell their performances to the fans and to the promoters, using invective and insolence to call on the fans to respond with cheers and jeers while proving to the promoter that they can carry a match, put themselves and the other guy over, generate the heat that will guarantee them a return engagement.

While wrestling is perhaps the only sport that loses credibility in the transition from amateur to professional practice, aside from very new or very young spectators, almost every fan assumes that professional wrestling matches are fixed to some degree, that the struggle between winners and losers is only a show, and that what they are seeing is a performance, a fake, not "real." Its funky costumes and props, fancy footwork and posturing, outrageous rhetoric, scenarios that conflate soap opera with carnival, and ceaseless marketing all mark professional wrestling as a theatrical and television spectacle more than as an athletic contest. Yet although professional wrestlers work "in character" and wear costumes, carry props, and deliver scripted challenges, and although they win and lose not by contest but by the promoter's decision, they are not actors per se. Rather they are genuinely strong, exceptionally skilled athletes, for the most part, whose performances supersede conventional expectations of "fake" and "real."

More than a vulgar parody of "real" sport, then, professional wrestling is also a sophisticated theatricalized representation of the transgressive, violent urges generally repressed in everyday life. More than a staged fight between representatives of good and evil, at its heart is a Rabelaisian carnival, an invitation to every participant to share in expressions of excess and to celebrate the desire for, if not the acting upon, transgression against whatever cultural values are perceived as dominant and/or oppressive in everyday life. More than an elaborate con game in which spectators are seduced into accepting the illusion of "real" violence, wrestling activates and authorizes its audiences through a series of specific strategies. Instead of leaving passive onlookers in the dark, wrestlers, through their physical and theatrical play, make their spectators complicit in the performance.

Professional wrestling's celebratory appropriation of the signs of both sporting and theatrical performance practices produces a parodic effect that is ultimately self-referential. Echoing Eco and Baudrillard, it seems obvious that professional wrestling must be understood as simulation, a hyperreality in which "obedience and transgression [are] equivalent" (Baudrillard 40). Wrestling's carnival sensibilities may seem "to belong to the people, liberating, subversive, because it gives license to violate the rules," but in the end it must be also recognized that this effect, "the moment of transgression, can exist only if a background of unquestioned observance [or at least knowledge of the rules] exists" (Eco 275). Professional wrestling, as it presents audiences simultaneously with the image of the real and with an idea of the fake, offers them, in Baudrillard's words, "a kind of thrill of the real, or of an aesthetics of the hyperreal, a thrill of vertiginous and phony exactitude, a thrill of alienation and of magnification, of distortion in scale, of excessive transparency all at the same time. The joy in an excess of meaning, when the bar of the sign slips below the regular water line of meaning" (50). Underlying professional wrestling's staged combat, as Baudrillard recognizes in commercialized representations both of everyday life and of war, "What no longer exists is the adversity of adversaries, the reality of antagonistic causes, the ideological seriousness of war—also the reality of defeat or victory, war being a process whose triumph lies quite beyond these appearances" (70). It is, therefore possible, in the study of professional wrestling, to recognize as Eco does in other low-cultural artifacts, the "instances where the American imagination demands the real . . . and to attain it, must fabricate the absolute fake; where the boundaries between game and illusion are blurred, [where] the art museum is contaminated by the freak show, and falsehood is enjoyed in a situation of 'fullness,' of *horror vacui*" (8).

Professional wrestling is frequently criticized in the mainstream press as a crude, brutal sport that lacks even the honest combativeness of a genuine contest, and indeed, at its worst, pro wrestling features a simplistic display of male bravado, exaggerated phony violence, and cultural clichés that often border on the fascist, and it is rightly accused of pandering for dollars to the lowest level of its audiences. But professional wrestling must also be recognized as a thoroughly entrenched part of American culture at all levels, with events televised into and performed live in almost every community across the country, potentially seen by almost every American at least once at some point in their lives. Indeed, any time I've mentioned my research in the past six years, no matter what the context, even now in New Zealand, I've received an immediate and generally excited response, laughter coupled with intense curiosity, and always the question: "It's fake, isn't it?" People of all backgrounds, classes, aspirations, and occupations have shared their memories of superstars and high-profile matches. Many men in particular have confessed to an earlier period of hard-core fandom, with wrestling fantasies forming an important bridge from childhood, the illicit pleasures of watching wrestling and of fanzines hidden under the bed an important part of the transition into adolescence and more explicitly homo- or heterosexual desiring.

While professional wrestling is not accepted as a legitimate sport—nor, obviously, can it be considered legitimate theatre—it does in fact intersect, exploit, and, finally, parody both forms of entertainment. The outrageous, idiosyncratic costumes, the ongoing televised taunts and challenges, and the live, largely pantomimed, confrontations are only the most visible theatrical characteristics in a fast-paced play of conflict and (ir)resolution. The actual language of wrestling in performance and training ambiguously combines both ends of the sport/theatre spectrum along with the jargon of the carnival con man. The wrestling event is often called the "show," but the lineup, as in boxing, is termed the "card." The locker room may at times be referred to as the "dressing room," but the wrestlers' costumes often are referred to simply as "get-ups" or "outfits." Their shoes—very soft patent leather lace-ups—are specifically designed for the sport, but in general they put their own outfits together, at least until they hit the superstar level, where support may be offered from professional designers. Indeed, for several years, the WWF employed a full-time designer, primarily to create backdrops for "offstage" events and personal props, but also to advise on costumes. This designer, Bil Mikulewicz, came to the WWF with an M.F.A. in theatre design from the Yale School of Drama as well as with an extensive background in scenic design for stage, film, and television. As he told me, even the locker rooms the fans see on television are often constructed as theatrical flats, most often because the actual locker rooms in the arenas as they tour are either too small or not photogenic enough (interview 1993).

As in the film industry, wrestlers are called "talent" and accumulate "credits," and success is determined by a perception of charisma and stage presence rather than by any sort of athletic point system. The audience's response during performances is recognized as the "heat" or "pop" provoked by the wrestlers. Highly visible superstars, such as Macho Man Randy Savage and Hulk Hogan, are given weekly television exposure as well as lucrative advertising and merchandising contracts. As in the stage, film, and television industries, however, more numerous are the players in the regional circuits who lack national recognition but are often well known to their intensely loyal local constituencies. As is typical of these other performance industries, the path to stardom is first perceived and imagined by the aspiring professional from the distant, mediated position of fan, then approached via hands-on training and apprenticeships with more experienced performers. The aspirant's actual chances of success—of performing outside a small local circuit, of even earning a living without having to maintain a day job—remain marginal at best.

Professional wrestling jargon is threaded throughout with the language of the con game. Most wrestling performances are considered "works," both in the sense that the wrestlers should be "working" to please the audience and in the sense that one wrestler in particular "does a job" to "put the other guy over." This "jobber" (often referred to in current fan parlance as "JTTS" or "Jobber to the Stars") must work to put on a good show, a convincing display of the desire and potential to win, in order to make the other wrestler—either a star or a new wrestler that the promoter wants to "push"—look good to the fans. Given that the professional wrestling performance is largely improvised, the potential always exists for a "shoot" in which the plan is forsaken, an accident occurs, or a genuine conflict erupts with the violence spilling over from display into actuality.

Performances are constructed according to the "logic" of the game, both in the sense of the display—a blow delivered must be given its due by the recipient—and in the sense of the way in which characters, conflicts, and story lines are developed in individual matches and over time. Often a promoter will attempt to generate heat for a rematch between stars by staging a "screwjob" in which the finish is disrupted or left unfinished—perhaps because of interference by other wrestlers or the referee's being knocked unconscious. All participants, including fans, present others with at least a bit of a "kayfabe," a term which is taken from nineteenth-century carnival, medicine show, and sideshow practice and simply refers to a con or deception. Kayfabe can also, less pejoratively, refer to participants' self-promotional, rhetorically inflated, and somewhat truth-obfuscating patter that resembles that of the talkers at the traditional sideshow. A kayfabian, then, is a con artist; most wrestlers are proud to be called kayfabians because it means they're in on the (con) game.

It is important to acknowledge that although the finishes of most matches are fixed in advance by promoters, and actions may be discussed and agreed upon by wrestlers before entering the ring, the individual matches are not choreographed or rehearsed as such. Rather performances are improvised, constructed moment-to-moment from sequences of moves according to traditional patterns and scenarios that are decided in advance. The wrestlers, promoters, and officials with whom I have spoken are adamant on this point, even as they concede that many wrestlers can be found in the locker room or the bathroom before matches talking through the moves. In the professional wrestling event a tension is always precariously maintained between the promoter's desire to control the show as a "performance" and the fan's desire to experience the breakdown of that control. Fans can be particularly contemptuous of overtly "staged" events at the same time that they take pleasure in predicting the shape of a match as it unfolds. Given that during tours cards featuring the same lineups may be repeated from city to city perhaps twenty times with only limited variations, patterns of action may be set down in a way that eventually appears rehearsed—especially to the hardcore fan (Brisco, interview 1993). It is in fact possible to sit next to fans at matches who predict outcomes with astonishing accuracy, based in equal parts on their knowledge of wrestling's fundamental conventions and, in recent years, on posting of match descriptions and outcomes on the Internet.

The history of professional wrestling in late nineteenth- and early twentieth-century America verges on the folkloric, a story passed along verbally much as the practice is from one generation of wrestlers to the next. In the version presented by Johnny Rodz and echoed by others, professional wrestling in the United States began with the strongman at the circus sideshow: "There was always a big guy with a guy behind him saying, 'Anybody come up and stand up five minutes with this guy gotta put up a hundred dollars, and if he wins we'll give him so much.' And you know, here is a *monster*. Who's gonna come up and wrestle with him—maybe some guy's drunk—but I betcha by the end of the night if it's a hundred dollars they'll have five hundred dollars." The exaggerated character of the wrestler was part of his stock-in-trade, a self-promotional device to draw the crowds and build a reputation that would precede his entrance into the town: "He could have some kind of costume, he could call himself Mr. Atlas, but he'd 've had to be some kind of monster. He knew he was taking his chances. There's always a big monster out there. Guys came in, put money up thinking they could take that guy. And it all started that way. Then the next minute, instead of doing one guy they did two guys, then they did four matches, then five matches, and now, today you have the major league deal" (interview 1989).

To this day professional wrestling exhibitions are rooted in ideas of community, filling a range of venues from the high-profile and enormous Trump Plaza and Madison Square Garden to the high school auditoriums, playing for profit and for charity. Even at its biggest, in the big leagues of the WWF and the WCW, professional wrestling stays close to the community, its superstar tours resembling the annual visit of the circus or the Broadway musical road show with their advance hype, the marketing of stars and products, and most of all, its elaborate glitter and pageantry. Clearly, the genuinely competitive sport of wrestling, if it ever existed at the "professional" level at all, must have rapidly given way to a consciously and conspicuously constructed spectacle in which the object was not so much to win a contest as it was to attract audience attention. From the beginnings of modern American wrestling, the wrestler had to make a show and be a showman in order to make an income and be successful. As a result of their day-to-day dependence on spectator interest and response, professional wrestlers were, and remain, showbiz entrepreneurs, hustlers who fought each other for spectator and promoter support as much as for victory in the ring.[4] Wrestlers today will say that while they are very proud of their strength and prowess, their real business is to generate heat, to get the spectators expressively worked up so that the promoters will hire them again and again. It doesn't matter if they're hated or loved—indeed, heels often pull a bigger "pop" than faces—as long as they're not received with silence and indifference. By providing what the spectators want, tickets and trinkets are sold, and fortunes may be made.

The emergence of the promoter directly influenced the development of professional wrestling's dramatic conventions. Johnny says: "What happened was that as the years went by there were guys who were looking and saying, 'Gee, those two guys out there killing each other, why can't I talk to these guys and make a show out of it or something, or make money out of it? And maybe I can hold these guys back and promote them a little better, put Atlas in this corner and Tonto in the other corner and be sure that I build up both corners so that this way people can pick on choices.' And before you know it, you had the crowd on this side on the part of the other guy." The promoter's job, then, became to build an event that would provoke a passionate response in a committed, repeat audience. As promoters took over the game, wrestlers vied for choice spots in the circuits by augmenting their performances with more attention-getting behavior and devices. In Johnny's words: "The promoters are out there watching the people watching the wrestlers. So they figure, 'Hey, this guy here, maybe he should be a little rougher' or maybe he starts pushing the guy into a position where the guy has to go over there and do a little more for the promoter's sake [like give an attitude]. Or maybe, 'I'll give you some money if you go over and yell at a couple of people' " (interview 1989). In turn, promoters found themselves in competition with each other not only for audiences but for the most charismatic wrestlers. The degree of hype surrounding professional wrestling today is a testament to the all-encompassing competitiveness of the game.

No matter how big or small the circuit, the promoter is in the most powerful position, and the more territory "owned" by the promotion, the more power the promoter has to attract and manipulate wrestlers. Says Johnny, whose own career in the WWF was largely in putting other guys over: "Promoters are like pimps. If one girl has her corner and the other one says, 'You got a fair corner, I'm gonna beat you out of this corner,' and she knows how to do it, then the pimp is gonna say, 'Hey, sweetheart, you take this corner and you better go take another corner.' He has them both so it doesn't matter." As the person who hires and fires, who decides a wrestler's place on the card and who doles out the paycheck as well as the prize money, if there is any, the promoter buys the wrestler's performance. As a result, it is the promoter who has the power to dictate who wins and who loses—and on what terms. "It's been like that since the world was born. And if a guy says, 'Look, I'm gonna put your name in lights up there, but I can only do it if you really mess this guy up or double-cross or something.' You either sign a contract for that or you're a fool. So, one way or the other you have a doggie doggie time" (interview 1989).

In fact, Johnny insists that there are times when promoters will just let the wrestlers go at it—"shoot the match"—to "find out who has the better spot, so they can judge it." The wrestler is also somewhat protected by the protocols and etiquette of the ring, which call for wrestlers to take turns being top man. But a wrestler is, in the end, the only man he can count on in his corner: "I go in there myself with all the credits I have and let Mondo [a bigger, younger wrestler] take it, for instance. I'd better have a good contract with the guy that runs the show [if I'm going to let him take it] and make sure that I have more action going for myself. It's a credibility problem. In this game it's a doggie doggie world and if you don't watch yourself, somebody is going to make sure that you look lousy so they can take your place" (interview 1989). While Johnny clearly means "dog eat dog" here and elsewhere, he says "doggie doggie" in what ultimately seems like a wonderful pun: clearly in his view wrestlers are like little dogs who will eat each other given the incentive.

That not all matches are fixed in advance is certain. At the August 1989 match at Gleason's Arena—promoted by Johnny Rodz with his then partner Steve DeVito as part of the NCW (Northeast Championship Wrestling) and ICW (Independent Championship Wrestling) circuits— the audience watched Mr. Nice's manager cheat Gino Caruso out of the Independent Junior Heavyweight title by shaking the ropes as he was about to finish his opponent off. Gino lost both his balance and the match. Afterwards, I followed him toward the locker room. His face was filled with anger and frustration as his friends and family surrounded him. In contrast, the following Monday when Mr. Nice (I never learned his actual name) showed up at the gym to work out, he beamed with pleasure as he was congratulated by Rodz and the others, telling us that he had worn the championship belt all weekend, even sleeping with it on. His pleasure was as (apparently) genuine as Gino's despair had been three nights before.

Promoters and wrestlers alike are keenly aware that professional wrestling's appeal is intimately connected to the immediacy of improvisation as well as a barely suppressed sense that the violence could erupt, veer out of control at any moment. What is presented in performance is still the illusion, if not the actuality, of a contest, a fight that is first and foremost rooted in the display of physical virtuosity. The wrestlers' training and performance always focus on ways of maintaining an effective relationship with the audience. The rules of the game—that each wrestler appear to be winning for a time, that good guy oppose bad, that the action should threaten to overflow the boundaries—and its "logic"—the give and take of the moves, the ways in which characters are to be articulated in action, the way in which dramatic tension is created and resolved—work in accordance with long-standing traditions that integrate athletic prowess and dramatic sensibility. Sequences of moves (sometimes called "exchanges") are learned and combined in performance according to traditional patterns that are both open and limited in the same way that patterns of movement in chess are circumscribed, and composed improvisationally much in the same way that commedia dell'arte once was. The action is fast and dangerous. A wrestler must know both the moves and the game in an absolute, reflexive way to be both safe and successful. Says one local promoter: "There's a thousand and one holds and a thousand and one reversals and ways to get out of it and get into it, and you have to be sort of a chiropractor in the ring—you have to know the anatomy. When you're fighting someone you have to know where to grab them, how to grab them, where to hurt them and where not to hurt them, and it's very, very rough—especially when you've got twenty-five to thirty thousand fans screaming, yelling for blood" (DeVito, interview 1989).

At its most visible level, then, professional wrestling performances are structured as a kind of contemporary psychomachia, or morality play. Strategies and structures are premised upon the confrontation between the "good guy"—in wrestling circles referred to as the "babyface," often simply the "face" or, sometimes, the "scientific performer"—and the "bad guy"—commonly referred to as the "heel" or the "rule-breaker." Whether in Madison Square Garden or in the local gymnasium, an audience will rarely see a face face a face or a heel a heel. The only exceptions arise when a promoter is testing a couple of wrestlers to see how they might play relative to one another and in relation to the spectators, or as part of a scenario in which a wrestler is in the process of "turning" from face to heel or vice versa, or when the fans' response to a particular wrestler runs counter to his self-presentation. Any ambiguity in the presentation of types and conflicts would seem immediately to violate wrestling's ethos and disrupt the audience's sense of community, and the fans take as much pleasure in expressing their outrage at divergences from the rules and logic of the game as in applauding its fulfillment. It doesn't matter whether or not the outcome is fixed in advance, although it usually is. The familiar patterning of virtue and vice, of loss and recovery, of victory justly or unjustly snatched from the jaws of defeat, of revenge for previous atrocities, along with the opportunity to play with and to judge the playing and players as they perform, seems to satisfy the audience in the same way that a favorite story (or play or movie) never fails to excite and reassure.

As such, it was not enough for Hulk Hogan simply to challenge Macho Man Randy Savage for the championship belt. Hogan's desire for the title had to be justified by Savage's elaborately staged, extended heel turn. Savage reoriented himself from his position as an excellent technical wrestler who played by the rules, a deserving champion with good on his side embodied by the pretty and loyal Miss Elizabeth, to a position as an untrustworthy brute by falsely accusing both Miss Elizabeth and the virtuous Hulk Hogan of betraying him. As he became more irrational in his verbal and physical attacks on his former companions, he also became both aggressively hostile to the spectators and a rule-breaker, using increasingly unethical strategies to win his matches. In the weeks before *WrestleMania V,* Savage was calling the Hulk's supporters "pukesters" and proclaiming himself the better wrestler (and the better man) because he stood apart from the audience, unlike Hulk Hogan who spent the same period emphatically assuring his fans that he was counting on them to support him in his hour of need. The heat generated by this conflict and the antipathy that was generated toward Randy Savage in particular was especially visible at a match in Madison Square Garden several weeks after the MegaPowers exploded, when a man dressed in an elaborate Macho Man costume circled the audience several times, attracting such a vehemently negative response that he seemed at moments to have placed himself in physical danger.

A climactic event such as the confrontation between the MegaPowers is achieved by careful structuring of the action in individual matches, in live events and in series of events, by building from verbal to physical, from small to large, and from slow to fast. Matches are thus pyramidic in structure. They begin slowly, almost daring the audience to grow restive, with opponents alternately circling and feinting at each other and shouting at the audience. The initial sequence of action can contain many pauses, extended holds and standoffs that are often deliberate al-

Macho Man Randy Savage challenges the audience from the top rope at
Madison Square Garden.

though sometimes accidental in frustrating the spectators' desire for action, inciting cries of "boring" or once at Gleason's memorably, "This ain't no love affair. Let's see some blood!" (2 December 1989). Gradually building to a climax with ever more frequent turnarounds between opponents, the action accelerates quickly from the last reversal to the final pin. The overall wrestling exhibition also follows this pattern, beginning with matches that employ less well-known wrestlers who are being either auditioned or pushed—that is promoted into greater audience awareness—by the promoter. These early matches serve as an audience warm-up for matches between stars, culminating in the "main event" in which the evening's biggest stars battle for belts. Earlier confrontations are limited in time to perhaps twenty minutes or less and are linked by interludes during which the announcer alternately urges the audience to buy souvenirs and to "stay tuned" for the evening's big matches. The main event closes the evening and may be scheduled for a full hour's duration. The individual components of the evening are both hierarchical and reflexively reinforcing: the slow opening, the gradual intensification of action, and the final rush to the finish create a cycle of anticipation and

A fan dressed as Macho Man Randy Savage provokes the audience just before being escorted from the arena by security.

reward, of desire and gratification, designed to seduce and sustain the spectators' ongoing investment.

The basic format of each individual match is similarly orchestrated. It begins with the wrestlers' entrances, which may be elaborate in the case of superstars, or almost invisible, as in the case of a "jobber." Wrestlers use their entrances to establish their characters and to define their relationships to the audience. The face circles the ring, exchanging high-fives with spectators in the front rows, inviting and receiving their gestures and words of encouragement. In the ring he welcomes the cheers of the crowd and lets everyone know that their support will be vital to his success. He performs for and with the audience, urging us to clap along with him, to chant "U-S-A," to applaud a trademark preparation ritual, to wave our souvenir versions of his gimmicks, and/or to mimic his characteristic gestures—a particular swing of the arms or a rallying cry. A master at working the audience, such as Hulk Hogan, may take ten minutes or more before and after his matches to perform muscle-man poses, which the spectators often mimic both to show their identification with him and to incite him to perform more directly for them, and to make a show of cupping his ears to hear the cheers.

Fans greet Macho Man Randy Savage as he enters the arena at the WWF's
Monday Night RAW.

In contrast to the way in which the face attempts to provoke or coerce
the audience into expressions of support, the heel enters and immediately confronts the spectators' jeers with his own insults, pointing and
shouting as they give him "thumbs-down," and otherwise displaying
both attitude and body in ways that are calculated to draw heat. At the
height of his heel phase, Randy Savage would stand on the top ropes at
each corner of the ring gesticulating his contempt for an audience that
performed its outrage with equivalent vehemence. Each wrestler may be
preceded and/or accompanied by managers, valets, and/or spokesmen,
many of whom will, like the wrestlers, take time to perform their own
relationships with partners, opponents, and spectators. As the ring fills
with players, the referee appears to caution each about the rules, and the
combatants generally spar with each other both verbally and physically
before the bell rings. As this grandstanding is taking place, the announcer gives the terms of the match: typically the time limit (if there is
one) and the number of falls required to end the match (usually one), as
well as any special conditions—for example, if there is a belt at stake or
the contest is a steel cage match for which opponents will be locked in a

fourteen-foot-high cage without a referee and proceed to fight their way out. He then announces the names of the opponents with their weights and places of origin, and he identifies their associates if there are any. The bell rings, and the match officially begins, although the fighting may have already commenced.

During the match each opponent has at least one period of time in which he appears to be close to victory, only to have the situation reversed. Almost always there is an extended period leading to the final reversal in which the loser-to-be will appear sure of winning, with the victor-to-be apparently on the verge of succumbing. The most skillful wrestlers seem to know exactly how far to push a potential loss or victory in order to make the reversal resound with the audience. In the match between Hulk Hogan and Randy Savage, for example, Hogan rode a crescendo of spectator chants as he raised himself up out of Savage's apparently invincible choke hold and quickly finished him off. Alternatively, the face may appear to be winning when the heel (generally with the help of his associates) cheats his way to an upset victory. It is this pattern of near loss and last-minute recovery, and of near win and last-minute loss, that gives the wrestling performance its essential dramatic tension and provides for a final payoff—the celebration of earned victory with the good guy or the condemnation of a stolen win against the bad guy.

A professional wrestling match may be described in conventional dramatic terms. There is a central conflict between two people (usually, but not always, men) representing distinct moral poles on terms easily communicated to and recognized by the spectators. Each articulates his stance in an alternating series of pre-event verbal attacks (in the WWF and the WCW these are televised) and physical confrontations (again televised by the big leagues, but staged over time in live performances regardless). These pre-event events can be carefully constructed as scenarios, designed in advance to shape the audience's perception of the characters involved and to establish the terms of the conflict in detail. Or they can be more accidental, responsive to a promoter's sense of the shifting winds of spectator allegiances or an inspired moment of improvisation by a wrestler eager for a better shot or a sense that the original plan isn't playing as well as expected. Regardless, the tension of the conflict between two or more wrestlers is developed over time, building to the actual live bout, a climactic event that ends either in tragedy—the bad guy wins by cheating—or in celebration, the latter a comic reassurance of the good guy's—and, by extension, the audience's—righteousness.

A match rarely ends with the final bell. Bad guys are never good losers and often assault the victor even as the referee holds the good guy's hand in the air. Conversely, if the bad guy has won by cheating (how else?), the good guy either will attempt to exact justice on the spot or will grab the microphone from the announcer to issue a new challenge. The story told is of an apparently unending cycle of violence. Each event contains within it the seeds of the next. In the symbolic universe of professional wrestling, conflicts are perpetuated through the performance of transgression—against the rules, against the boundaries, against justice—and apparent violations by one or more of the heels threatens to rend the social fabric as represented by most visible rules of the ring. The hero is compelled to defend the community's integrity, but often finds himself marginalized in the process, forced to step outside the rules himself to meet the enemy on his own corrupt terms. Circumstances create a necessity; the rules must sometimes give way to moral imperative, but always at a cost. Almost always the hero—as Hulk Hogan demonstrated at *WrestleMania V*—displays and overcomes his suffering as a public testament to his great effort on the community's behalf.[5]

There are effectively two sets of rules: those made and presented so that they can be visibly broken and those that actually govern the performance of the game. In fact, the only official rules—at least in the guide published by the New York State Athletic Commission—prohibit eye-gouging, biting, and close-fisted punches (225.11). These and other basic rules are readily ignored, and the referee frequently seems unable to halt the constant violations of the rules by players on both sides. He is easily sidetracked by another wrestler or distracted by a devious manager as an illegal move is performed by the bad guy. Even though, or perhaps especially because, he is (in most states) hired from an athletic commission roster and consequently acts as the most visible representative of official authority, the referee becomes another actor in the play of good and evil, a role that he generally enacts as deliberately as do the other participants, arguing with wrestlers and spectators alike as they challenge his authority. Indeed, it is not unusual for promotions to include at least one "celebrity referee" in big events, as when Mr. Perfect appeared at *WrestleMania X* (WWF 1994) to officiate at the title match between Lex Luger and Yokozuna.

As with other elements of wrestling, the role of the referee is only partly connected to sport. According to Johnny Rodz, the referee was originally introduced into professional wrestling by promoters not simply to regulate the violence but more particularly to pace the spectacle so that the audience would see more than just two men trying to kill each other (interview 1989).[6] In current practice, the referee steps in to break up a clench that has lasted too long, and he frequently frustrates the spectators' desire for closure by stopping the count at two, compelling the wrestlers to resume sparring. Above all, within wrestling's dramatic structure, the referee's inadequate efforts to prevent or even see the heel's rule-breaking provides justification for the otherwise virtuous hero to step outside the rules and reassert order.

Like the referee, the ropes are frail boundaries, ineffectual as containment for the conflict, inevitably failing to prevent the violence from spilling off the platform and into the audience. The apparent violation of the most visible restraints serve to generate heat by bringing the action close to the fans and creating a sense of danger, which is sometimes reflected and reenacted in the skirmishes between spectators. Conversely, an off-

The referee attempts to stop Bam Bam Bigelow from attacking Virgil in the corner at the WWF's *Monday Night RAW*.

duty wrestler or group of wrestlers may intrude from outside, crossing into the ring to disrupt the orderly progression of a match and sparking a brawl that may then spill from the ring into the audience. Then too, one of the primary tropes of the wrestling match is the chase around the ring on the floor as the referee impotently threatens to disqualify wrestlers for crossing the ropes.

The crossing of the ropes, the pursuit of an opponent after a victor has been declared, the punch in the face to the referee, all seem designed as a display of out-of-control violence, a way of generating heat, and a proof that matches might not be as scripted as the fans assume. It is tempting to see the brawl as an attempt by promoters and wrestlers to make the "fake" look "real." But although the heat generated in such moments may certainly be genuine, what is effected is a comic, carnivalesque revel in which the audience may participate—if only vicariously. As the wrestlers break free of the ineffectual authority—the rules, the ropes, the referee, the bell—they become more surrogates than scapegoats for the audience as they enact a representative rebellion against other impositions of social order, those found outside the arena.

The wrestling arena thus offers its audience a site for sanctioned transgression of everyday proprieties. Spectators may participate in the performance by shouting challenges at the wrestlers and the referees. They catcall and carry on, one-upping each other's jeers and cheers as, laughing with pleasure, they look around at friends and neighbors for approval. But the same agreement that prevents wrestlers from actually harming each other during the give and take of a match also extends to the audience. Being "in on the game" means accepting certain unspoken limitations. With few exceptions, actually storming the ring or intervening directly in the conflict is generally unthinkable even for the most engaged or enraged spectator.

Although the heightened competition for star wrestlers has brought with it inflated paychecks for a select few, big-money superstars are still relatively exceptional, and few professional wrestlers make a full living from wrestling alone or can expect a lifetime income solely by performing. Indeed, the hustle for gigs and for ways of making money from the game never ends. Many wrestlers, like Johnny Rodz, perform multiple roles both simultaneously and over time: a professional wrestler for close to thirty years, much of them with the WWF, Johnny has operated his school for wrestlers for many years and also promotes matches in more local circuits. Moreover, most—like Johnny Rodz and Captain Lou Albano—started their careers as fans. Captain Lou, for example, saw his first professional exhibitions while in the service in 1953. Those who pursue careers become first wrestlers and managers but must either support themselves with other jobs or turn to ancillary forms of marketing and (self)promotion: in Captain Lou's case, a Nintendo-sponsored daily syndicated cartoon show, a fiction series published by Zebra Books entitled *Body Smasher,* a 900 telephone number offering wrestling news, and so on (interview 1989).

Each participant in the wrestling event has a role to perform: from the wrestlers, referees, and managers to the TV commentators, the judges, doctors, ringmen, and spectators. Many of the men on the sidelines have been wrestlers themselves; in fact, all managers in the state of New York, as in many other states, must be licensed and insured as wrestlers (*Special Rules for Wrestling,* 225.09). Most participants in the local and regional circuits hold other jobs to support themselves while wrestling whenever and wherever possible, either as they pursue the brass ring of stardom or in order to earn a few extra bucks while they more fully participate in an activity they love, the game. The same is true of the more peripheral participants: Judge Julius Deak, presiding at ringside with Reverend Paula Mora at Gleason's Arena (18 August 1989), offered his thirty years of experience around the wrestlers' ring as a paradigm. A supervisor (now retired) at a dental supplies company (now bankrupt and out of business), he began his career in wrestling as an usher, became an inspector for the New York State Athletic Commission, and now serves as a judge at Gleason's and elsewhere (interview 1989).

Whatever their position in the game—from aspiring novice to full-fledged star, and from wrestler to ringman, even hard-core fans who contribute to photo exchanges and bulletin board discussions on the Internet—participants are visibly and vocally proud of their insider status. For the fans in particular, knowledge of the rules and language of professional wrestling marks them as members of a self-selected elite. They are the privileged participants to whom wrestling's performers cater. It is the spectators whose participation in the event is essential to fulfill the performance objectives, objectives that are largely economic. Simply put, every move in the arena, every spoken word and every pose, explicitly and implicitly supports the commodification of the spectacle. Spectators are repeatedly urged to purchase products: T-shirts, mugs, ice cream sandwiches on which the wrestlers' trademarked images have been imprinted, foam rubber two-by-fours (in imitation of Hacksaw Jim Duggan's signature prop), foam rubber fingers and headscarves imprinted with Hulk Hogan's "Hulkamania" or Randy Savage's "Macho Madness," autographed posters, souvenir programs, and "official" magazines. At the same time, upcoming live events, the television programming, and even movies featuring the superstars, especially Hulk Hogan, are pushed.

In exchange for this endless marketing, the promoters and wrestlers work very hard to give spectators their money's worth. The extravagance of the costumes—shiny satin and sparkling sequins, feathers and full-body caveman suits—and the exotic props—big live snakes and colorful parrots, 20-foot-long steel chains and exaggerated barber's shears—together with the promise of a display of violence that at any moment might veer out of control, overwhelm the referee, overrun the barriers, exceed the official time limit, and enter the audience, all signal the eagerness of the players to excite and please the audience. All are calculated to keep the spectators spending money and coming back for more.

A wrestling event is conspicuously constructed around a set idea of what the wrestling audience wants and expects to see. To be a successful professional wrestler is to be able to manipulate your opponent and your audience at the same time. To be a successful promoter is to arouse spectators' desires and expectations by creating a context—an angle or story line—for which the witnessed confrontation becomes simultaneously the payoff—the climax we've all been waiting for—and a setup for a new story line to be spun out in the coming months. For example, the title bout was barely over at *WrestleMania V* when both opponents issued fresh accusations and challenges, the conflict between Randy Savage and Miss Elizabeth culminated several years later in a staged wedding at *SummerSlam '91,* and Hulk Hogan and Randy Savage have continued to square off, most recently in the WCW. At every point of contact with the audience, the audience is reminded of its primacy: the wrestlers always keep one eye on the crowd, competing for spectators' passions and inviting them to play along.

A public wrestling event at Gleason's Arena was to a WWF exhibition at Madison Square Garden what a school play is to a Broadway musical. The contrast began with the size of the audience. Gleason's seated perhaps five hundred people, but matches rarely drew more than three hundred spectators to the monthly matches. In contrast, the WWF regularly

WORLD WRESTLING FEDERATION®

MONDAY, JULY 30, 1990
BRENDAN BYRNE ARENA
EAST RUTHERFORD, NJ

MAIN EVENT: DEDICATION MATCH — ONE FALL, ONE-HOUR TIME LIMIT

HACKSAW JIM DUGGAN		EARTHQUAKE
Glens Falls, NY...280 lbs.		Vancouver, B.C., Canada...468 lbs.
&	VS	&
TUGBOAT		**DINO BRAVO**
Norfolk, VA...384 lbs.		Montreal, Quebec, Canada...260 lbs.

FOR THE WWF INTERCONTINENTAL TITLE — ONE FALL, ONE-HOUR TIME LIMIT

MR. PERFECT	VS	TITO SANTANA
257 lbs.		Tocula, Mexico...244 lbs.
(CHAMPION)		(CHALLENGER)

FOR THE WWF TAG TEAM TITLE — ONE FALL, ONE-HOUR TIME LIMIT

DEMOLITION		HART FOUNDATION
AX, SMASH		JIM "THE ANVIL" NEIDHART
&	VS	&
CRUSH		**BRET "HITMAN" HART**
Combined Weight...891 lbs.		Combined Weight...515 lbs.
(CHAMPIONS)		(CHALLENGERS)

HILLBILLY JIM	VS	THE MODEL RICK MARTEL
Mud Lick, KY...286 lbs.		Cocoa Beach, FL...234 lbs.

KOKO B. WARE	VS	THE GENIUS
Union City, TN...228 lbs.		Downers Grove, IL...252 lbs.

JUMPING JIM BRUNZELL	VS	HAKU
White Bear Lake, MN...235 lbs.		Isle of Tonga...273 lbs.

BRADY BOONE	VS	BROOKLYN BRAWLER
Oregon City, OR...221 lbs.		Brooklyn, NY...242 lbs.

WORLD WRESTLING FEDERATION®

WATCH WWF WRESTLING:

Saturdays	12 noon	WNYW-TV	Ch. 5	WWF Superstars of Wrestling
Sundays	12 noon	WNYW-TV	Ch. 5	WWF Wrestling Challenge
Lunes	11:00 pm	WNJU-TV	Ch. 47	WWF Superstars de Lucha Libre

WWF card.

Gleason's Gym, Johnny Rodz School of Wrestling
—PRESENTS—
★ A Christmas Wrestling Special ★

SAT.-DEC. 2 ★ 8:00 P. M.

GLEASON'S ARENA 29 FRONT ST. BROOKLYN, N. Y.

★ ★ MAIN EVENT ★ ★
A RETURN GRUDGE MATCH

JOHNNY RODZ
vs. IRISH CHAMP

DAVEY O'HANON

★ ★ TAG MATCH ★ ★
HILLBILLY Cousin Luke & The Bird Man vs. Mondo Kleen & BIG SWEET William

★ ★ SPECIAL TAG EVENT ★ ★
The Rhino Power vs. The Headhunter With Magic Jack

★ ★ 6 MAN TAG GRUDGE MATCH ★ ★
Mr. Nice, Jr. Champ & Kid Krush Mgr. The Captain
vs. Tommy Norton & White Wolf, Manager Frankie Longo

★ ★ PRELIMINARIES ★ ★
TOMMY DREAMER vs. MIGHTY MARK ADAM

DIESEL DON vs. THE SOUTHERN GENT

TONY COCO T vs. THE REBEL

THE SHADOW vs. BRIAN DRESCHER

Price $10.00 ☏ Telephone: (718) 797-2872 - 9570 - 338-9765
B. Q. E. Exit 28 Cadman Plaza, Under The Bklyn. Bridge, All Subway
Stop's 2 Blocks Away High St./Clark St./Borohan/Court St

Gleason's Arena card.

fills the twenty-thousand-plus-seat Madison Square Garden. The atmosphere at Gleason's was a cross between county fair and farm auction, with families making up a large percentage of the audience. For the most part, children were seated in the front row with the women, while the men sat together at the sides, occasionally scolding a child who got out of line or asking their wives to bring them another beer. Between bouts, the children would practice fighting in the aisles as the men and women chatted amongst themselves. The officials—two judges, a timekeeper, and a doctor—sat at a folding table at the edge of the audience area. Familiar to each other and to many in the audience, they would visit with one another, slap each other on the back, and generally catch up on gossip.

The action at Gleason's was smaller, slower, more homegrown and less polished, certainly, than in the big leagues. But this was not necessarily a liability and, indeed, its roughness and genuine sense of community contributed in large part to its appeal. New wrestlers—some with as little as two months' training—went in first in short, fifteen- to twenty-minute bouts, and there were often lengthy, unexplained delays between matches that were relatively silent, not filled with scripted hype and displays of products, unlike the WWF's events. At most events, the referee would end the evening by warning the final contestants that they were reaching the curfew of 11 P.M., at which point the wrestlers would quickly resolve their matches. But although events presented by Johnny at Gleason's always had their awkward moments, the close proximity of the audience appeared to heighten their engagement with the performance. The immediacy of the action, the sense of discovery in the younger wrestlers and playfulness in the more experienced ones, created an energy that was highly infectious, irresistible really, and intensified the "friction," the heat experienced by the spectators.

Because of their venue's obvious limitations, the Gleason's Arena promoters generally offered at least one match that pushed the boundaries of the conventional match, something the audience couldn't expect to see at Madison Square Garden—for example, a twelve-man tag team or a "Mexican Freestyle Street Fight." The rules for the latter were remarkably complex, but, in brief, two boxing gloves were placed in the center of the ring; at the bell, the wrestlers began to fight for the gloves; once a wrestler had secured a glove on his hand he had to knock the other man out for a count of ten and then pin him for a count of three. Not exactly a piece of cake. But regardless of such elaborations, the basic performance values—the funky costumes and props, music, violence spilling into the audience, the hero's narrow victory and the villain's ill-gotten win—were faithfully maintained. The Romanian Warrior carried his battle ax, and the Little White Wolf entered in full rain-dance regalia. Tag-team partners Rhino Power #1 and #2 were led into the arena by their manager, the Captain, who kept them tethered by their neck collars to a chain until he could no longer keep them from the ring. The regulars in the audience knew which wrestler to cheer and which to jeer, and the newcomers picked up their cues with alacrity. In 1989, predictably, the Russian got the loudest and most vehemently negative response, particularly from the children who approached the ring in packs to shout "U-S-A!" and "Russia sucks!" as he yelled "Fuck you!" back at them.

In fact, wrestlers at Gleason's Arena were always well-schooled in generating heat, especially as heels. Mr. Nice, in white tuxedo and tails with "NICE" scripted in silver across the seat of his pants, alternately smirked at and shunned the spectators on his way to the ring. Larry Brisco performed a vivid heel turn by rejecting tag-team partner Little White Wolf,

The Captain leads Rhino Power #1 and #2 into the ring at Gleason's Arena. The Russian welcomes them in.

Little White Wolf greets the fans as he makes his entrance at Gleason's Arena.
One of his opponents, the Cuban Savage, stalks him from the ring.

shaking hands with and offering his team's trophy to their opponents at
the match on the 22 April 1989. Larry went on from this match to add
"Crazy" to his name, and was subsequently challenged by his disgruntled
former partner, who has become even more popular with local fans for
having been betrayed. Years later, Larry remembers the way in which
this story line originated and then deviated from its planned climax: the
Rhinos had the trophy and needed to move it in order to generate heat.
They only had the trophy in the first place because they had sold one
hundred tickets to the match, and they figured that with a strong angle
they could sell two hundred tickets to the next match. Larry teamed with
Little White Wolf for a few matches to establish their partnership. Instead of taking the trophy as planned and continuing as a face, he followed an impulse in the ring and went for the juice of a heel turn. While
surprising the others and winning a great deal of animosity for himself
all around at a point when he was still relatively new to the game, he also
got a huge boost from the performance and to my surprise remembers
the event vividly, as I do, more than four years later (interview 1994).

It's easy to antagonize an audience. Generating heat as a face generally takes more skill. Johnny not only regularly showcased his students in these matches, but he demonstrated both his athletic prowess and his ability to generate heat by being genuinely "Unpredictable." In the April 1989 contest against Cuban Savage #1, he took a beating at first but rose up against not only the Savage, but the Savage's two companions, who had in best heel tradition been illegally aiding their friend and hitting Johnny when he was down. Johnny chased them all from the ring, grabbed the announcer's microphone, and, climbing through the spectators over and on the auditorium's chairs, issued challenges in Spanish and English. He worked the audience for ten minutes or more in this way, while everybody cheered, clapped, and stomped, and his students stood in the back of the room transfixed.

Later, in an August tag-team match, the Cuban Savage and his associates threw salt in Johnny's eyes, temporarily blinding him and drawing spectators more quietly to ringside in concern. When I asked him about the incident on the following Monday, he simply (and evasively) answered that it is the way the game is played. Was it his idea? Did he know he was going to have salt in his eyes? He wouldn't say, but shrugged and indicated that it was necessary to do such things to spice up the action and spike spectator response (interview 1989). Seeing him on occasion warmly greeting and fooling around the ring with the Cuban Savage and his friends, it was obvious that regardless of how the confrontations between them were planned, a high degree of personal trust provided for a greater range of antagonistic expression between them in performance.

In contrast to the rough intimacy of a community-based wrestling event, the WWF wrestling performance has two distinct, carefully orchestrated components. The first are the matches themselves. The second, upon which the marketing of matches has come to depend, is syndicated television programming that is explicitly designed to create and sustain the audience for the live and pay-per-view matches. Programs such as *Wrestling Challenge* and *Superstars of Wrestling* splice together footage from the WWF's house shows with verbal commentaries and filmed set pieces that introduce and develop characters in short vignettes. Along with *Monday Night RAW*—a WWF innovation in which matches are presented in more intimate arenas and, at least in its first years, broadcast live—these programs serve to generate heat and ticket sales for the WWF's shows around the United States and for big annual events such as *WrestleMania, SummerSlam,* and *Royal Rumble.* It is worth

The Blue Blazer drop-kicks Greg "the Hammer" Valentine from the top rope at a
WWF match in Madison Square Garden.

noting that in addition to broadcasting its own equivalents—
Championship Wrestling and so forth—the WCW has recently taken on
the WWF by positioning its own version of *RAW,* called *Nitro,* directly
against *RAW* on Monday nights, thus creating a macrocontest for the
fans, who now heatedly compare ratings numbers alongside face turns in
their newsletters and bulletin board discussions.

In the big leagues, the television programming provides the setup,
the live event the payoff. The first provides an ongoing narrative—the
words—the second the action. As such television programming has become the essential tool of the promoter. It allows him maximum control
of his circuit's image and impact, the power of the editor's splicer all but
eliminating the instabilities of improvisation. More important, it provides a space in which narratives may be developed in detail, both
through the episodic sequencing of images over time and through the
close-up in which the face or heel can tell his story to the audience either
through a commentator or directly. Lacking the immediacy of the local
audience and the volatility of a performance that is always to some degree
improvised, television is an ideal medium for marketing the promoter's

product: the challenges that justify the violent confrontations are issued and the status of grudges announced in ways that can be rehearsed and reproduced, thus ensuring that the audience will hear and see what the promoter scripts. The marketing effort is ultimately self-reflexive, with the live action in the arena accompanied by frequent exhortations to spectators to watch the television programming where they can see the action up close and hear the wrestlers speak.

In general, the WWF and the WCW sponsor two types of live events, both of which are videotaped and offered either free to the viewer in the syndicated programs or on pay-per-view terms via cable. The first type of live event happens in local arenas all over the United States and features the superstars in contests against each other as well as against relative unknowns, many times local "stars" hired for the match to lose to the national star. These temporary "jobbers" ("sacrificial victims" might be more appropriate) may in fact consider this work a "tryout" for the big leagues. Regardless of the outcome—and such wrestlers are rarely offered contracts beyond the match—putting the superstar over gives them an opportunity to generate heat for themselves locally and to acquire a bit of the superstar's aura at the same time. The second type of event is the superstar exhibition, major annual events that are generally reserved for presentation in top-line venues such as Madison Square Garden and broadcast only as pay-per-view, heavily promoted in advance and internationally marketed as videos and souvenirs afterward.

For both types of events the work of the cameramen, commentators, and announcers, as well as the wrestlers, is to create images that transcend the medium of television and communicate the vitality and volatility of the live event directly to the spectator at home. Multiple cameras are positioned in the arena, hand-carried from the center of the ring into the audience and back, and even suspended directly over the ring for a bird's-eye view. The potential for star-making in the 1980s and 1990s has, consequently, increased dramatically since the time of Gorgeous George, extending well beyond the wrestlers themselves to managers and hangers-on, notably Mr. Fuji, Slick (the Master of Style), Colonel Jimmy "Mouth of the South" Hart, Bobby "the Brain" Heenan (also called "Weasel"), and of course Miss Elizabeth. Even the promoters and their stand-ins—especially Vince McMahon of the WWF—have come to be recognizable as "stars" with whom the fans have an ongoing, albeit not always appreciative, relationship.

The live event is always contextualized and its audience primed by ongoing television presentations, which deliver story lines in ways that resemble nothing so much as soap opera, albeit in a masculinized voice. Indeed, the astronomical growth in the popularity and visibility of professional wrestling is largely the result of a shift in the style of television presentation pioneered by Vince McMahon in the early 1980s. The earlier more resolutely deadpan and straightforward broadcasting of events has been replaced by a progressively more sophisticated imitation of other mainstream television forms. Not only do wrestling programs appear to parody the "straight" sports coverage of programs such as *ABC's Wide World of Sports* or the Olympics, with their tongue-in-cheek updates, their cheeky interviews, and their own (comic) cast of sportscaster characters, who are themselves former wrestlers still in the game sparring verbally and, on occasion, physically: Lord Alfred Hayes, Gorilla Monsoon, Mean Gene Okerlund, Jesse "the Body" Ventura, and frequently Macho Man Randy Savage. They also borrow heavily from soap operas, MTV, and *Entertainment Tonight,* producing their own versions of these genres as parodies that both complement and critique the mainstream culture as a kind of low-culture postmodernist romp.

The superstars of wrestling are well-polished performers who—like actors coming from summer stock and regional theatres to Broadway and Hollywood—have acquired their veneers by working their way up from the smaller circuits. Their sharply focused performances, slick styles, and clearly articulated, carefully controlled characterizations reveal not only their years of experience but also the unifying power of the WWF and WCW promotional machinery. The Ultimate Warrior, who (we are told) comes from "parts unknown," races to the ring and circles it several times before leaping onto the platform and shaking the ropes. His televised challenges mimic and mock comic-book "Indian" rhetoric: "As I rise from the darkness, I set aside no time for fun and games or recreational periods. I cannot live by what you tell me to do. I do what the warrior wants and the fear I see in your eyes has begun to blossom" (*WWF Superstars of Wrestling* broadcast, 1 July 1989). Hacksaw Jim Duggan struts to the ring with a two-by-four in one hand and an American flag in the other, frequently turning to the audience and, with a thumbs-up gesture, shouting "Ho-oh!" Boris Zhukov brings his Russian flag into the ring and, in a big league version of the Russian's performance at Gleason's, tries to intimidate the spectators into singing "the Russian national anthem" along with him. Macho Man Randy Savage dresses like a cross between a cowboy and a '60s biker in sunglasses, tie-dyed shirts, sequins, and headscarves. Entering to "Pomp and Circumstance" and facing the audience from the top rope in the corners, he punctuates his lines with "Yeah!" and can barely force the word through his clenched teeth. In contrast, Hulk Hogan looks like nothing so much as an aging blond surfer (hometown Venice Beach) as he enters to "Follow the dream of America," rips his T-shirt off and tosses it and his head-band to the spectators. He invariably spends ten minutes or longer encouraging his fans as they cheer and mimic his muscle-man poses. He calls his fans "hulksters" or "little hulkamaniacs" and on television exhorts them to follow the "three demandments: training, prayer, and vitamins."

Some wrestlers, like Savage and Hogan, remain reasonably constant, their fans apparently resistant to any radical shifts in personae, for example: Bret and Owen Hart, Mr. Perfect (Curt Hennig), and Jim Neidhart (who now advertises a wrestling school on the Internet). Others develop characters that can change remarkably over time. Shawn Michaels began with the WWF as a face, acrobatically tag-teaming with Marty Janetty as a "Rocker." But for some years afterward he has been a successful heel, exchanging his brightly colored Rocker togs for heavy-metal black leather, chains, and earrings, strutting into the ring to the strains of "I'm not your boy-toy" and gum-snapping as he swings his hips in the center of the ring before taking on the audience. Conversely, Lex Luger first appeared in the WWF as "the Narcissist" at *WrestleMania IX* (1993) at Caesar's Palace in Las Vegas with a bevy of beautiful, barely dressed showgirls who held shields as mirrors that reflected the desert sun blindingly as he removed his silver lamé robe and flexed his overdeveloped muscles. Then a year or so later, having pushed his heel status to the limit, he turned face by bodyslamming the apparently unslammable Yokozuna—a Samoan-American, who is presented as a non-English-speaking Japanese Sumo-brute—on the Fourth of July. In order to take even more advantage of American sentiment against the Japanese, this last event was staged on the former World War II aircraft carrier *Intrepid,* which is moored in the New York City harbor as a tourist sight. After various WWF stars and heroes from other sports such as football attempted to lift Yoko in vain, Luger landed in a helicopter, strode across the tarmac dressed in blue jeans, boots, and an American flag jacket, lifted Yoko, and slammed him, subsequently announcing that he would no longer wrestle only for himself but now for "all of America" before taking off in the "Lex Express," a chartered bus that toured the United States for the next month or so.

A gimmick may be owned by a wrestler or by a promoter: at Gleason's one afternoon the rumor circulated that the Undertaker gimmick was purchased by the WWF for $75,000. Moreover, certain characters may be performed by a number of wrestlers: for example, Doink the Clown has been performed by five or six different men over the four years of his existence, and indeed one hard-core fan activity is listing the wrestlers who have appeared in his particular guise. In general, however, a wrestler's character is so clearly intertwined with his identifying artifacts—especially in the context of the relentless marketing efforts of the WWF and the WCW—that when one wrestler takes another's props as trophies they come to take on a narrative and semiotic life of their own. These props may remain constant in the values they represent—power, danger, sexual heat—but in the semiotics of the ring come to be characters themselves in the wrestlers' ongoing self-reflexive parodies. Hacksaw Jim Duggan remained a fan favorite as he became "King Hacksaw" following a victory over King Haku in which he appropriated Haku's gimmick. At a "coronation" attended by other WWF good-guy superstars, Duggan displayed his booty, the crown, cape, and processional entrance music of the former king as he claimed the title. The crown then passed to Randy Savage, who proclaimed himself the "Macho King" at another "coronation" attended by the WWF's roster of bad guys.

Similarly, the superstars' wrestling moves, especially their finishing holds or pins, become signatures, identified as such with their characters. Hulk Hogan always finishes with a leg drop. Rick Rude calls his finish the "rude awakening." Bad News Brown twists his opponent's head with his feet, calling the move the "ghetto blaster." Honky Tonk Man takes his opponent down for the count from behind, twisting and turning him into the floor in what he calls the "shake, rattle, and roll." And Brutus "the Barber" Beekcake pantomimes going to sleep as the audience cheers before finishing with the "sleeper" (a choke hold) and cutting locks from the now unconscious loser's hair—perhaps as a kind of masculine Delilah to the loser's Samson, although Brutus somewhat surprisingly wrestles as a face. These finishes are also markers and mediums of exchange; owned by one wrestler, a finish can be displayed by another as a sign of the ultimate victory and insult, as in *WrestleMania X* (20 March 1994) when Shawn Michaels appropriated Razor Ramon's "Razor's Edge": "The Ultimate Insult!" exclaimed commentator Jerry Lawler, "finishing him with his own move!" In this case, Michaels was unsuccessful in using Ramon's move, signaling a double failure; in the end, perhaps only the virtuous Ramon was powerful enough to prevail with the "Razor's Edge."

Always visible in the well-lit arena and in the sweep of the camera, the fans perform for each other as they perform with the wrestlers. The audiences for professional wrestling come to appear as integral to the staged event, playing their part in the performances as cued. Spectators learn how to behave at the live matches by watching the TV shows, which are explicit both in providing surrogates, models, and cues in the form of close-ups of audiences and in telling spectators what is expected of them. While the commentators express joy or dismay as events unfold, the wrestlers address television spectators directly with signature phrases through the camera both in studio shots and as they enter, exit, and circle the ring for their matches. "No mercy!" shouts Bad News Brown as he strides from the locker room. "Poultry in motion!" crows the Red Rooster.

Whatever the venue or card, what is visible on television and in the arena are spectators who are fully involved and apparently important influences on the outcome of matches and story lines. Beyond contributing their cheers and jeers, buying and displaying the products, and spreading the word through their own networks, the fans are always prepared to move the action along if it flags or if they are ignored for too long, with a loud, unified "Boring!" which brings an immediate response from the ring. As valued customers, the buyers of events and products, the fans are always the point of the performance. Ultimately, it is the fans' desires and their power, or at least the promoters' idea of what the fans desire and how they are powerful, that is constructed and displayed in the squared circle. It is indeed a "doggie doggie world" in which the contest is as much for fans as it is for belts and prize money, and in which the victor can truly claim to be "what the world is watching!"

Chapter Three

LEARNING THE GAME

It looks like a helluva game. It *is* a helluva game. But it's
very rough. It's not as simple as it looks. If it was that simple, every Tom, Dick, and Harry would be doing it.
—Johnny Rodz

Once you start training, you're a professional.
—Chris Moniz

"You wanna wrestle? Or you wanna fight?" Three wrestlers are
at the center of the ring at Gleason's Gym on a very hot, very
humid Saturday afternoon (25 June 1994). After several hours
of patiently drilling a couple of newcomers on the basic moves—falling
backward and rolling forward, a simple hold and reversal, a takedown—a
few of the more experienced wrestlers have been playing out scenarios
and roles. They have been alternating as opponents and referees, taking
turns at winning and losing, acting as faces and heels and discussing
role-playing in general for about thirty minutes. But in what for the
moment still appears to be the customary give and take of the wrestlers'
workout, the tone has shifted almost imperceptibly, and now it appears
that Larry is genuinely angry and potentially violent. No one, neither
Tommy and Chris who are with him in the ring nor the other wrestlers
lounging beside me on the sidelines, is quite sure how serious the conflict

is, how dangerous it is becoming. The air in the gym is suffocating, everyone sweat-drenched.

Larry challenges Tommy again, walks away, then turns back, threatening, as Tommy follows him to the corner in an evident effort to smooth things over: "I'm not gonna slap you 'cause I'm *angry*. I'm gonna slap you to teach you a *lesson*. You keep getting in my face, *nobody* here is gonna blame me for what happens next. Not these guys . . ." He strolls over and points to the other men. "Not Sharon . . ." He points to me, pulling my attention up from my notebook in which I am recording the discussion about role-playing and forcing me to maintain eye contact with him. Somewhat taken aback, I prevaricate: "Well, I don't know, Larry, maybe . . ." I'm not fully certain if this is part of the game, or if we're now choosing sides for a serious brawl. I definitely do not want to be on the wrong side, and as usual, after I speak it's not at all certain that my answer has sufficed.

Tommy and Chris continue their attempts to reason with Larry, to smooth things over, but I can't hear much. Whatever it is that they say,

"You wanna wrestle, or you wanna fight?" Larry challenges Tommy and Chris.

it obviously fails to placate, and after about ten minutes, Larry explodes. He grabs Tommy, who of the three has the least wrestling experience, and throws him across the ring into the ropes, butting him, tossing him, and periodically pinning him. Helpless to stop the attack and increasingly agitated, Tommy tries to maneuver, to catch his breath, gain a foothold or scramble away. But Larry dominates him with apparent ease, so that no matter how Tommy moves, Larry stays draped on top of him. At one point, they tumble toward us at ringside. We quickly back away, and the newer wrestler is pinned a few inches from me, face down, belly across the ring's edge, his legs bent all the way back at the knees as Larry sits on them holding the ropes both for greater leverage and, I assume, in order to inflict a certain amount of pain along with the humiliation.

Johnny Rodz strolls out of his office and stands, grinning, at ringside as the rout continues. He urges Tommy to figure it out, to reverse the situation and regain control by scooting his hips out from under Larry. Chris takes up this attitude of the coach from inside the ring. But the fight—for now a fight is surely what this is—doesn't end until Larry releases Tommy, who immediately stalks away to a far corner of the gym where he remains visible beyond the other apparatus, pacing at the windows that overlook the street. Larry then turns on Chris, but the fight between them ends abruptly when Larry drops the smaller man on his head in what appears to be a genuinely dangerous pile driver. Larry takes off for the showers, pausing briefly on his way out of the ring to discuss barbecue plans for the Fourth of July with Johnny.

Chris sits on the mat, evidently dazed and in pain, rubbing his neck. Mohammed, another newer wrestler who has been watching from ringside, jumps in and massages Chris's neck for a moment, then gives him a playful chop, which earns him a few sharp words. He backs off. The others drift away, gather their belongings, confirm their workout schedules with each other, and generally say their good-byes. Johnny warns another newcomer that he will not be accepted in the ring in street shoes and as the youngster struts away mutters about the Walkman the kid is wearing. Clearly this newcomer is not yet demonstrating enough seriousness for Johnny's liking.

Mohammed offers to join me in the walk to the F-Train and the ride back to the City, and after a short conversation with Chris, I accept. On the sidewalk I ask Mohammed to explain what happened in a way that I, as an observer and woman, can understand. But beyond averring that

Larry was teaching Tommy (and Chris) a lesson in "respect," and recollecting his own injuries—to body and ego—from similar "lessons," he seems unimpressed and unconcerned. As we board the train our conversation drifts to his feelings of pride now that he can take part in showing newer wrestlers the ropes, and on to his day job and his hopes for a career in professional wrestling. Clearly, from Mohammed's perspective, and that of the others, today's confrontation was simply the way things work when one is learning the game. While this event was more explosive and extended than many, it is in fact true that I have seen the men turn against each other in this way a number of times in the years that I've come and gone from ringside. It's what Johnny calls "getting your face pushed to the mat" and as such is an essential part of a wrestler's initiation into the culture of the ring and a masculine rite of passage. Some men walk away after this lesson in respect. The ones who return for more, Johnny says, have earned the right to be "let in on the game" fully (interview 1993).

To learn the game an aspiring professional wrestler must do more than acquire athletic and performative skills. He must also assimilate masculine codes of behavior. That is, he must master two distinctive sets of vocabularies and rules all the while earning the right to enter and perform in the squared circle. Newcomers like Tommy and Mohammed sign up and begin training in large part because they are captivated by the same fantasies of masculine prowess and dreams of stardom that those who are successful come to sell to an audience. But learning the game is an often brutal reality check, an enforced encounter with one's own physical, intellectual, and emotional limitations experienced through the tedium of repetitive practice and the volatility of the other men. It is an exercise in managing the self, as much about learning to submit as it is about dominating, and about learning to accept the demand that one lose as it is about enjoying the pleasure of winning, or at least the appearance of winning. The lesson is vital because a wrestler who aspires to professional status must come to terms first with other wrestlers and then with the power exercised by the men who dominate the game. As with many other masculine rites of passage, it strikes me as supremely ironic that to prove their manhood wrestlers must first surrender it to the others.

For many years, Johnny Rodz has owned and operated the Unpredictable School of Professional Wrestling Training Center. Johnny offers training over time in "the art, methodology and skill of professional

Johnny Rodz watches a workout from ringside.

wrestling."[1] His claim to expertise is based on his own more than thirty years of experience, including long stints in the World Wrestling Federation. Johnny is a stocky, visibly muscular man in his early fifties. Standing next to him at odd moments, I am surprised at how big he really is, accustomed as I have become to seeing him among taller men. In large part, I have come to understand that the reason my impression of the amount of space he takes up varies with each encounter has much to do with the contradiction between his gentleness, especially with me and with the younger men, and his intensely concentrated physicality.

Originally from Puerto Rico and proud of his climb into middle-class comfort and respectability, Johnny does not make a full living from his wrestling enterprises. Rather he works irregular hours for the New York City newspapers, inserting sales flyers for union wages. His story reflects that of his students: he saw wrestling first as a young fan and began wrestling as part of his effort to escape poverty and marginalization in New York City. He tells me that his success in the WWF also led to his downfall, hinting at a profligate period in which the usual forms of excess predominated. Now, declaring himself older and wiser, he is rightly proud of his reputation as an exciting, "unpredictable" wrestler who can manage both his opponents and the spectators to his own advantage with an astonishing combination of sheer energy and forceful control. At his matches, the spectators are exuberantly enthusiastic, chanting "John-ny! John-ny! John-ny!" until long after he has left the arena. Understandably, he is conservative with his students, self-consciously a guardian of their integrity as well as his own and that of the game.

What Johnny teaches new wrestlers are first the basic athletic skills: how to fall backward and roll forward, the holds and moves, as well as the combining and sequencing thereof. At the same time, he offers ongoing lessons in performance and showmanship: how to create a character, how to act the face or the heel, how to relate to an audience, and above all how to generate heat. While his approach to training is direct and engaged, he also utilizes an each-one-teach-one strategy. In a linked chain of apprenticeship, the more experienced wrestlers, some with as little as two or three months' training themselves, come to act as trainers and coaches to the newer ones, going a few rounds, demonstrating moves, offering advice from the sidelines. What underlies and informs all of these lessons, regardless, is an ongoing lesson in respect, in giving ground as well as taking it, in both humility and masculine pride. It is

Johnny demonstrates a hip toss with Mohammed (pages 56 and 57).

an initiation that, in Victor Turner's terms, may be seen to "humble people before permanently elevating them" (25). Like Tommy, Larry, Chris, Mohammed, Vito, and all the other wrestlers at Gleason's, including Johnny, every professional wrestler, from the jobber to the most successful star, has undergone a version of what Johnny teaches, a process of assimilation via discipline and submission into the wrestlers' fraternity.

The lessons are thus transmitted from generation to generation, with Johnny Rodz acting as the primary transmitter and guardian of the secrets of professional wrestling in ways that resemble the processes by which many other performance practices, theatrical and sporting, Western and Asian, are inculcated in the young.[2] In truth, the way in which wrestlers come to the Unpredictable School of Professional Wrestling and the process by which they learn the game from Johnny and the other men seems to be as much like the way in which young hopefuls flock to Hollywood or New York and embark on learning the trade of acting in movies or on stage from various veterans of the business as it is like other forms of sports training. Like neophyte actors, what neophyte wrestlers buy is more than a chance at a dream; it's a chance to live in the dream while working toward it. When a wrestler enters the ring he begins to "act as" a professional wrestler. As he deliberately works at developing a wrestler's physicality and assimilating a wrestler's knowledge, he acquires a distinctive wrestler's presence. The wrestler he becomes in practice becomes his persona in performance.

As in other sports training, Johnny is more than a trainer or coach. He is an important role model and sometime father figure to younger men who, beyond their dreams of stardom, often seem hungry for the community of the ring. In addition, Johnny is usually a new wrestler's first promoter and agent. He often produces his own events and also organizes cards for other promotions that take place in gyms, community centers, high school auditoriums, and fairgrounds throughout the northeastern United States. Many of these events are actually fund-raisers and charities, and the wrestlers earn a minimal amount of money per match— generally around one hundred dollars—depending on how prominent they are on the card and what additional roles they actually play. He has also helped to organize a number of international tours, creating opportunities to take his wrestlers with others to the Caribbean, Japan, and the Middle East. And when a wrestler seems ready, he helps him get gigs elsewhere, including the chance to "audition" for the big leagues, especially the WWF.

When I began my research in 1989, the school was housed at Gleason's Arena, a vast warehouse space planted directly under the Brooklyn Bridge in an industrial neighborhood. When I returned in 1993 after a two-year hiatus, the arena had become a parking garage, and the school had moved down the street several blocks and into Gleason's Gym, which is world-famous for the boxers who have trained there. The first thing I see when I leave the desolate industrial street and climb the stairs to Gleason's Gym at the second floor is a banner with an inspirational quote from Virgil: "Now, whoever has courage and a strong and collected spirit in his breast let him come forward, lace on the gloves and put up his hands." Manning the door is Cal, who has been at Gleason's in one way or another for uncountable years and who is always willing to share his stories about Gleason's history of famous boxers as well as his own poetry. Cal invariably welcomes me warmly with a "Hello there, young lady!" and tells me which wrestlers are around in the office or the ring. Unlike the arena, most of the gym is set up for boxers. In contrast to the relative openness of the arena, the gym is cluttered with low rings, mats, punching bags, weight room, chin-up bars and exercise bikes, and mylar "mirrors." Locker rooms and offices surround its periphery. From the doorway, the only athletes visible are boxers: sparring with and without coaches, hitting the heavy bag or the speed bag, shadow-boxing.

But one of the four rings, set up in the far corner, is distinctly different. It is Johnny's ring, transported from its original home at the arena to the gym. Instead of four ropes, it has three that appear thicker, more thoroughly wrapped with colorful tape, and somehow softer than those in the boxer's rings. Its platform is visibly cushioned, with a layer of foam covered by well-worn soft blue canvas, and supported from below by a large, coiled spring. The turnbuckles are also carefully covered with foam and fabric. It is in this ring, and on the cement floor surrounding it, that the wrestlers work and hang out when not drifting in and out of Johnny's office, where the walls are covered with yellowed newspaper clippings, cards and posters from past matches, autographed pictures of famous (and not-so-famous) wrestlers with and without Johnny, and family snapshots.

The boxers and wrestlers work separately for the most part, although they greet each other in passing and, on occasion, will spar playfully in keeping with the ongoing half-joking half-serious debate about the relative merits of the two athletic arts. Aside from the two or three women who regularly train as boxers and Sky Magic—who is the one woman I see training consistently with the wrestlers over the years—the room is thick with men. In contrast to the wrestlers, who cluster together in and around Johnny's ring, the boxers work in pairs or solo in what often appears to be a very fierce, private circle of concentration. The noise is often overpowering. Leather gloves pound leather bags, announcements are made over the barely audible PA system, the phones ring, and bells and buzzers continually sound off with no apparent logic. At odd intervals, the room is abruptly silenced, apparently in response to a bell or buzzer. The boxers mill around for a bit. Then the bell rings, and the noise resumes at its former level.

For three or four days each week the wrestlers add their loud bumps and expressive yells to the general cacophony of the cement and cinderblock room; and on Saturdays several "Mexican Wrestlers" often join the workout, practicing and sharing with the others the more acrobatic, complexly and explicitly choreographed art of Lucha Libre. The contrast between the highly interactive community of wrestlers and the singularity of the boxers is immediately evident. Where the boxers appear self-absorbed, their trainers and sparring partners subsumed within the individual's effort, the wrestlers congregate inside the one ring, in a ringside corner, or in the office. As they come and go throughout the afternoon, they greet each other, shake or slap hands—or, in a gesture I've seen nowhere else, swipe one or two fingers—exchange news and gossip along with the occasional video, and watch earlier arrivals working out before stepping into the ring themselves. While two wrestlers spar in the center of the ring, others take turns tagging in or acting as referees, and playing spectators. Except for the newest of the newcomers, each wrestler frequently exchanges advice with the others, demonstrates holds and falls, and explores optional moves. As a result, despite the aggressive rhetoric, the antagonism and grudges that are the vernacular of public performances, the atmosphere during workouts is generally genial, more expressive of a strong sense of community and family.

Wrestling hopefuls hear about the Unpredictable School of Professional Wrestling primarily by word of mouth, although articles listing

Tommy steps in to offer advice to the new wrestlers working with
Mohammed and Chris.

training venues appear periodically in fanzines. About ten to fifteen wrestlers work out with Johnny regularly. Newcomers, many of whom fail to return after the first few weeks, tend to trickle in one or two at a time, although Johnny's recent induction into the WWF Hall of Fame has given the school a tremendous pop. In general, the new trainees are young men in their late teens or early twenties, longtime wrestling fans eager to become full-fledged participants without much idea of what that might entail beyond what they've seen live and on television. Because they are themselves fans, they come in the door having already internalized a lot of the language and behavior of the "squared circle." Most have participated in at least one other sports activity, especially football, and many have had experience competing as amateur wrestlers on high school and/or college teams.[3] A few, such as Mondo Kleen—who was briefly featured in a series of WWF matches as Damien Demento—I am told have come to wrestling from professional football, although later I learn that this bit of biography is a fiction. In addition, many are obsessive bodybuilders who have invested years (as well as a great deal of self-esteem) in developing their physiques, with some, including Sky Magic and the Little White Wolf, actually coming to professional wrestling directly from competitive bodybuilding. As is common in the big leagues, several of Johnny's trainees, notably Gino Caruso, have come from wrestling families themselves, although they are generally modest, quiet about the fathers, brothers, and/or uncles who wrestled before them. Many, including Vito and Chris, have even done some acting, at least at the community theatre level, and some, especially Vito, aspire to movie careers as well. Some, notably Larry, are highly educated; others have failed to finish high school.

When asked what has brought them to the wrestlers' gym, why they want to be professional wrestlers, most say, "It's fun" and leave it at that. Indeed, watching them pose as the stars, practicing attitudes along with the moves, it's clear that the desire to be like the stars drives most of them, and the pleasure of the fantasy remains intact in those who stay. Larry describes the pleasure of wrestling itself as a kind of "Zen," adding: "I like the lines, in the sense of skating or diving or like somebody hits a home run. The lines in your body, there's a perfection to it" (interview 1989). For Johnny, the attraction of the game remains located in the experience of personal power that extends beyond the ring: "Being in professional wrestling, it shows you could be in any kind of game.

That's the top of the line, when you can learn how to fall and be better than a stuntman in a movie. You know everything" (interview 1989).

What these aspiring professional wrestlers also have in common, aside from their love of the sport and fantasies of stardom, is that they have all seen Johnny Rodz wrestle and are suitably awed at the opportunity to train with such a star. Indeed, Mohammed recalls that seeing Johnny star in wrestling exhibitions in Trinidad had inspired him to immigrate to New York in December 1992 and, once there, to save enough money to pay the fee (interview 1993). Mohammed, who is sometimes called Indio by Johnny and the others because he is from Northern India via the Caribbean, is tall and dark. As time passes, he lets his hair grow longer and becomes visibly more muscular as well as increasingly graceful. He clearly considers it a privilege to be training with Johnny and is highly committed to learning the game, whatever it takes. He works very hard at whatever is demanded of him, arrives early, stays late, and persists in repeating the lessons offered long past the time when his peers have grown bored and drifted off.

The most experienced wrestler aside from Johnny is Larry Brisco, who has been a regular at Gleason's off and on for seven or eight years. A powerful and smart wrestler, who dominates everyone but Johnny in the ring with apparent ease, Larry is also the most well-educated of the regulars: an undergraduate degree from Wesleyan, a stint teaching high school social studies in New Jersey, and for the past few years a full-time job as a paralegal doing securities analysis on Wall Street, where he claims he startled the lawyers he worked for by looking like a dumb jock (a "stud" he says) while working at a high level of comprehension. He has wrestled professionally for several years and, as one of the first guys Johnny calls when he's putting together a card, is proud of being able to position himself as the smart guy or the dumb guy in the ring, as a babyface or heel, and of being able to put himself over to audiences using wrestling moves rather than simply posing (interview 1993). Indeed, he appears genuinely baby-faced and is solid without seeming particularly large or muscular. When I last saw him in June of 1994, he was working toward a Ph.D. in sports sociology at the University of Connecticut. While writing this book two years later, I track him down on the Web and learn that he is still wrestling and is now working on his dissertation: "Bloodsport, Manly Art, Sweet Science, and Boxaerobics: An Ethnography of a New York City Boxing Gym." Having come full circle, we begin the conversation again, albeit virtually. He shares his writing on wrestling with me for use in this book; in turn, I encourage him to pursue teaching and publishing in performance studies, and we discuss future collaborations.

At Gleason's, Larry can be taciturn and loquacious in turns. He is the only wrestler I meet who has read Barthes's essay, although he has professed himself indifferent to it. It is Larry who offers me insight into the "psychology" of the game, and it is Larry who defines, clarifies, and discusses basic pro wrestling terms with me: what it is to "shoot" a match, how a wrestler generates "heat" and the problem with "cheap heat," the "logic" of a match, how a wrestler positions himself as a face or heel, and so on (interview 1993). Regardless of his intellectual accomplishments, or perhaps as part of them, Larry is—as the event that opens this chapter reveals—a major player in the culture of the ring, fully committed to the game, and full of wrestler-attitude, at one point echoing Johnny and the others when he tells me that a boxer wouldn't last two minutes in the ring with him and neither would "real" (that is, amateur) wrestlers. When he works alone or with the others in the ring he never surrenders his awareness of the "audience," frequently making eye contact with me or demanding my approbation. It is Larry who actively demonstrates how smart a wrestler must be to play the game, how quickly action must follow thinking in the ring, how clearly the moves and the ideas governing them must be assimilated into the wrestler's kinetic memory.

Next to Larry, it is Chris who appears most successful in balancing his aspirations against what is possible. In part, this is owing to his being the smallest of the men there, perhaps 5-foot-6 at most. But it is also owing to the particular way in which he came to wrestling and his current life choices. Like Larry, he seems to walk the line between self-conscious machismo and a reflective gentility, which includes a genuine respect for, and ability to talk directly with, women. It is, in all probability, this last quality that leads me to make an exception to my usual rule of keeping distance from the men and to approach Chris for a meeting outside Gleason's. Over coffee at an Upper West Side café, Chris tells me his personal history, and we discuss the game of wrestling along with that of life (interview 1994).

Chris discovered wrestling at thirteen, becoming a fanatical fan: he watched the programs, went to matches, bought the magazines, and played at wrestling with friends. He also wrestled with the team as a tenth grader in high school, but quit after one and one-half years—both, he says, because the coach favored the bigger, more obviously athletic boys and because he suffered a failure of nerve, becoming somewhat timid about injury. After high school he joined the Marines and did some wrestling there. Finally, soon after his discharge on June 19, 1991—he remembers the precise date—he was riding the subway when he had a profound moment of recognition in which he realized that he still had the dream of becoming a professional wrestler. He found an article about wrestling schools in the *Slammer*, called around, and quickly landed at Gleason's, drawn by his memory of seeing Johnny Rodz wrestle during his teen fan years.[4] Less than two weeks after his epiphany on the subway, Chris met Johnny at Gleason's and started learning the game on July 1, 1991. His respect for Johnny as a wrestler, trainer, and man has only been enhanced through close contact. In fact, Chris speaks frankly of his feelings for Johnny as a father figure who both pushes and protects his protégés, and he now consciously, conscientiously makes a point of taking on the role of coach and model himself.

Chris is understandably very proud of what he's accomplished at the same time that he is careful to put forward his awareness of his limitations, what he has yet to learn. Recognizing that he must first learn the game as a wrestler, his goal is now to become a manager or perhaps a referee, although the latter is a very tight field. Echoing Johnny and Larry, he affirms: "Once you start training, you're a professional." Affirming what I've been told by everyone else, he adds that professional wrestling is as much an athletic and performance practice as it is an economic status, and he stresses the essential combination of athletic skill, business acumen, and performance awareness that makes a professional wrestler: "You can learn the physical and not get past being a fan, a mark—you can still not 'get' the game." When I push him on his definition of "getting the game" he prevaricates a bit but concedes: To "get the game" a wrestler must be able to "put himself over" but must also be able and willing to put the other guy(s) over. He adds: "Johnny Rodz spent most of his WWF career putting other guys over, but that didn't cost him respect of his professional standing" (interview 1994). In other words, putting the other guy over, jobbing, or losing on command is a key part of the game, not peripheral at all. A professional wrestler, he avers, has to be able to take the bumps and sell the moves, no matter what his position in the scenario and/or the promoter might demand. In Chris's view, a professional wrestler does the job as he's paid to do it.

In contrast to Chris's reflective summation of his training and career path, Vito is rarely without his bluster and always seems to be angling for a way ahead. Perhaps this is to be expected; at the time when he was most in evidence at Gleason's in 1993 and 1994 he was also highly visible professionally, getting a series of shots at the WWF, jobbing on *Monday Night RAW* as "Von Kraut," a neo-Nazi with his shaved head gleaming and various fascist emblems adorning his red and black Lycra. Like the other men at Gleason's, Vito is highly ambitious, only half-joking when he calls himself the "Skullster" and plays at the game in the ring. He is also the most intimidating, both big and volatile, leading me, especially after my run-in with his explosive temper, to keep a certain amount of distance. Vito is impressively graphic when he describes his initiation period, recounting with more glee than rue the numbers of bruises he accumulated when he started three years ago and the poundings he took—from Mondo and Larry in particular—until he learned respect for the others and the game (interview 1993). And indeed, in the ring he is highly disciplined and forceful, his intensely focused attacks on his opponents always in danger of stepping over the edge into genuine violence, in direct contrast to his occasional gleeful horsing around outside the ring.

It is surprising, then, especially given our past encounters, that Vito is the most direct in approaching me about the possibility of crossing over into acting. While it is obvious that much of his eagerness to break into film or theatre goes hand in hand with his undisguised desire for stardom, and especially for money and fame, he also confides in me that he has taken great pleasure in acting in community theatre productions: *The Wizard of Oz, West Side Story,* and at least one Shakespeare play (he can't remember the title) top his list. When I tell him that something like 1 percent of Screen Actors Guild members actually make a living wage acting, and that the actors in the production I'm currently directing off-off-Broadway are unlikely to be paid more than a token $25, he is openly appalled and contemptuous. Like the others, Vito is reasonably successful outside the ring, working as a manager for an import/export company where he is given what seems like remarkable autonomy and responsibility, as well as a few perks, including pickup games of basketball during his breaks (interview 1993). When I check back in two years later, I hear that Vito, having just returned from ten months of full-time work wrestling in Puerto Rico, is looking forward to further success as a professional wrestler.

The only woman to appear consistently at Gleason's over my five years of research calls herself Sky Magic (I never learn her real name). Well-educated like Larry and presenting herself at the intersection of a number of cultures, Sky is a sculptor who has a graduate degree from Parson's School of Design in graphic art and has worked commercially in the years since gaining her degree. At our first meeting, she explains that she felt trapped in her career and initially tried to make a go of competitive bodybuilding, but it's very expensive with little earning potential (interview 1993). Moreover, because her mother and sister are both competitive bodybuilders and karate experts, she wanted to work in an area that would be her own. Consequently, she has turned to wrestling in part she claims because of its superior cardiovascular workout: "better than aerobics," she says. More important, she hopes to be able to earn enough to quit commercial art for good. She is compact and very tightly muscled, executing an impressive number of chin-ups, alternating front and back holds, at intervals during her workouts. Her disciplined and eclectic approach to physical training is evident as she takes instruction from the Mexican Wrestlers when they offer it and even brings in a kick-boxer, Tony, for additional private training. She is also, like Vito, quite active in pursuit of paid work. She organizes for a "girl-wrestler" video and plays agent for other women. She is always gracious in greeting me upon my arrival and frequently urges me to try wrestling myself (she tells me she wants another woman in the ring, but I suspect it's part of an effort to redeem me from my hopelessly unfit state).

Sharing the ring with the American-style wrestlers are the practitioners (luchadores) of Lucha Libre or free-style wrestling, commonly referred to as Mexican Wrestling, usually Rubio and Frankie who have been partners for a number of years. As they always work in the ring masked, rarely removing them at the gym, it takes a while to come to know them and to be able to identify them. Rubio is a somewhat stocky man. Surprisingly soft in appearance, he is, like the other wrestlers, strong and agile, and moreover a remarkable acrobat. His age is difficult to guess, and the information he provides in conversation even more suspect than usual, especially his repeated insistence that he is married to a woman who, like me, is named Sharon and Jewish, with whom he

Rubio pins Frankie as they practice Lucha Libre.

has two children aged eighteen and twelve. Like the others he is curious about how my husband takes my hanging out with wrestlers and why I don't have children (interviews 1993). He frequently jokes around with me, telling one new wrestler, Jeffrey, that I am his "teacher" and Jeffrey had better behave himself because I'm tough and will take him out if he doesn't. Jeffrey is clearly baffled and lasts only the one session, never to return.

The other wrestlers, Johnny in particular, tend to be dismissive of the luchadores, in large part because of the way in which it is obviously choreographed, appearing almost balletic in performance. But to my less experienced eyes Rubio's skill and experience, as a man who has wrestled since 1972, seem evident from his exchanges with Frankie and the other wrestlers. Although he no longer performs, he continues to work out with Frankie and the others, practicing extended, apparently complex sequences of flips and turns and rolls. He also does a brisk business in masks, capes, and jackets, as well as long Lycra shorts. When I admire the strikingly beautiful patterns based on tigers and other animals that have been painstakingly stitched into the fabric, he tells me that he designs and builds them himself, charging between $50 and $100 depending on how elaborately constructed the item is. He is, like many of the others, very generous with me. After one long workout on a hot and sweaty afternoon, he takes the mask off his face and, after a discussion about his cottage industry in costuming other wrestlers and the power of the mask, gives it to me.

In contrast to Rubio's visible strength, Frankie is quite short and thin, which makes the cooperation between the two men even more evident. Frankie becomes the first man to greet me when I arrive at the gym, always breaking out of his workout to find a chair for me and bring it to my customary corner before resuming. He is as soft-spoken as Rubio is outspoken and very earnest about his workouts and his presence in the ring, whereas Rubio is more frequently playful and joking. It is Frankie who talks with me most seriously and eloquently about his relationship to his chosen mask—tiger with a red power dot on the forehead—which Rubio makes especially for him. He refers to it as a source of power and, like Rubio, claims to be unable to wrestle effectively when not fully masked and costumed. While Rubio insists that he loves his mask because he's "sexier" and "all the women" love him when he's wearing it, Frankie says that it's important to him that he is able to "do things—not just the moves" and that he feels he can act more forcefully and gracefully as a wrestler and a man when wearing his mask than when he is without it (interview 1993). And indeed, the masks of the luchadores have a striking effect. By supplanting the wrestler's face with a less human image—abstractions of animals and symbols of power—what becomes visible is the idea of the man and his body in motion. When Rubio and Frankie do work without their masks, they are not so much diminished as utterly transformed.

Because novices come to the school with stars in their eyes from so many years of being hard-core fans, of watching wrestling in whatever medium is available to them, they are already relatively fluent in the vernacular of the game. Much like starstruck acting students, what they most desire is to transform themselves from watchers to performers, to become insiders with the same gloss and dash of the superstars. At the same time that each longs to be close to and like their heroes, each is convinced that he is special, that he is marked for success, the one who will become a star in his own right. They want the fame with all that it promises, the aura and mana of "real" men. They want the money. They

Rubio wearing mask.

want the power. They want the girls. For the most part the ones who stick it out past the initiation period, as they keep their day jobs and continue to wrestle in their spare time, may become more realistic, even cynical, about their possibilities. Those who stay never quite lose the pleasure, the sense of privilege as they stroll into Gleason's, change into workout clothes, and step into the ring with the others. They linger together at ringside, exchange magazines and videos as well as information, compare notes about matches they've seen, and mimic moves and gimmicks, taking turns one-upping each other in imitating, for example, Macho Man's long-running commercial for Slim Jim: "Chips! I hate chips!" Vito postures from the ring, insisting that everyone call him the "Skullster"—a reference both to his shaved head and to Hulk Hogan— and riffing on Hogan's latest performances.

Time in Johnny's office is often spent telling tales and listening to Johnny tell stories of his years in the big leagues. The day after André the Giant died suddenly (29 January 1993), a group listens to Johnny reminisce about being paid extra by the WWF for about a month and a half to drive the Giant around and keep him company during his apparently legendary drinking binges, how the job came to an end because it was exhausting and impossible to police the other man's behavior in that way. The afternoon drifts by as Johnny tells his stories about adventures with the Giant and other superstars. Awe at Johnny's past and his storytelling is visibly intermingled with the urge to tell their own stories and the desire to have their own stories to tell, while the connection between the men feels at moments as comfortable as if it were a campfire gettogether.

Training at the Unpredictable School of Professional Wrestling is not cheap. Johnny is not easy to pin down on what he charges, but he does tell me at one point that his basic fee is three thousand dollars for unlimited access, in effect, a lifetime membership. This one-time fee is in contrast to what I hear anecdotally of other wrestling schools, in which trainees are charged big initiation fees as well as monthly membership charges.[5] The setup with Johnny ensures that he gets his money fairly quickly at the same time that it puts the onus of training directly back to the trainee. That is, as far as Johnny is concerned, once the money has been paid it is up to the individual to demonstrate his commitment by continuing to show up, by working out, and by responding positively and productively to instruction and criticism. Because no further monies can be expected, if a newcomer drops out after the first weeks, no one will call or otherwise attempt to entice him to return.

From Johnny's point of view, as well as from those who have stayed the course, the wrestler who signs with him gets what he pays for—whether it's a quick and painful reminder of the difference between fantasy and reality, or a long-term education in the art and ethics of professional wrestling coupled with membership in a fairly exclusive community of like-minded men. And each of the wrestlers, no matter how much or how little else they tell me of their experiences, describes the various phases of his/her coming into the game as a series of initiations and confrontations, of challenges met and surmounted. In the words of Little White Wolf: "When I first came here I was gonna quit. Because it's not easy. I've been here six weeks. I've been a bodybuilder, but I'm tight, so I have to loosen up a little. I've been thinking of taking a yoga class. [After the first day] I was so sore that to stand straight up to fall straight back, it bothered me. Or to have one of these guys come tumbling down on you . . . [laughs]. But the guys are beginning to work with me, so I'm learning a little bit better and I'm getting a bit more relaxed. So I'm going to stay here no matter what" (interview 1989).

The underlying values and processes of the wrestler's workout are, it seems, contiguous with the actor's or the dancer's workshop/rehearsal: concentration, precision, consciousness into subconsciousness, repetition, demonstration, explanation, imitation. Like student actors, student wrestlers must settle down for a period of repetition that is coupled with an enforced recognition of their limitations in the face of wrestling's physical, emotional, and intellectual demands. It is not as easy as it looks on television. Like actors and dancers, during their early apprenticeship they undergo moments of embarrassment and humiliation, periods of doubt alternating with renewed desire, earning kudos as much for their displays of discipline and determination as for their accomplishments. Like actors and dancers, the lessons often include heavy, painful demands on both body and spirit. That is, the learning takes place at an abstract level—in a coming to understand and be able to explain to others the concepts—which is only possible through an active engagement at the physical level, in the practice of doing. Like actors and dancers, while it is possible to become an insider in a very privileged community, a key component of the learning process is coming to recognize that very few "professionals" are ever successful enough to give up their day jobs.

Tommy demonstrates falling backward for a new wrestler.

The professional wrestler's education is first and foremost kinetic, an inculcation into the body of movement in parts and in sequences through seemingly endless repetition. Indeed, the first days and weeks of training can be astonishingly tedious, calculated in part, it seems, to convince novices that the game is a serious and difficult discipline in which the steps toward a finished performance must be painstakingly accomplished. A new trainee generally spends the first few sessions practicing three fundamental skills: falling backward and hitting the mat so that it resonates loudly with his fall, tumbling from standing forward in a shoulder roll to standing again, and propelling between the ropes. As the days progress, the wrestler comes to combine these three moves: bouncing from the ropes and tumbling forward to standing then falling backward; springing to standing, running at the ropes, and repeating the sequence. Often another wrestler will be positioned crouching on hands and knees so that the others are forced to spring over him as they tumble forward. In particular, the lesson in falling backward is surprisingly difficult for many novices, combining as it does a confrontation with an apparently primal fear of falling in this way with the intense tedium of repetition. These basic movements—like those of the dancer—are to become imprinted in the body's memory, a vocabulary of reflexes that can be summoned in workout and performance without the conscious thought of the wrestler. As such they are generally practiced by every wrestler when he enters the ring as a warm-up preparatory to the workout.

The pattern of instruction is remarkably consistent, and even at this apparently simple stage, the more experienced wrestlers will frequently step in and correct the trainees, demonstrating and remonstrating with them. Like Johnny, each wrestler is a potential teacher and role model, someone to whom another wrestler may look with admiration and respect as well as aspiration. At one workout (15 May 1993), for example, Larry spends time with a group that includes Sky and Mohammed, making them roll on diagonal and then run at the ropes: "You don't have to go fast," he tells them. "If you're smooth it creates a sense of action." He treats Sky and Mohammed to a lesson in the hip toss. When Sky seems ready to quit, he urges her on until she is successful. A little more than a year later (25 June 1994), I watch Mohammed coaching some first-timers for a while. Then Chris takes over, using much the same language to push a new guy to keep going: "It's monotonous, but you gotta do it to smooth the bumps." He gets the other guys to line up and tumble with the neophyte in part to diminish the guy's self-consciousness about being watched, and the others offer encouragement and advice: "You want to be ready to go when your opponent's coming at you." They take turns tumbling across the ring in a basic shoulder-roll, coming to a crouched ready position in the corners, then falling back and hitting the mat: "First thing you do when you come in," Chris says. "Over and over again. Two hundred times." Mohammed concurs.

Simultaneous with the effort to master these basic moves come less explicit lessons in spatial relations: how to find one's feet, how to remain aware of one's position in the ring—the center versus the corners—and relative to one's opponents, how to sustain one's balance and the proper posture at all times, how to step into the basic stance from any position, how the feet should be positioned, how flexed the knees should be kept, and so on. By the second or third week, most newcomers enter the gym and immediately begin to tumble across the ring, pivoting to stand and face an imagined opponent from the corner, then crossing the ring again in a fluid, almost trancelike sequence of repetitions. Often they are set up in opposing corners, so that they cross the center alternately in a kind of perpetual motion machine that is disrupted only when one man stumbles and breaks the rhythm. With the tumbling, then, comes awareness of the positioning of others in the ring and the first opportunities to face an opponent, if only obliquely or in the imagination. As he tumbles to the corner, the new wrestler will now stand facing out and then immediately fall backwards (or forwards), always hitting the mat for effect. Practice at circling and lunging comes to lead to a headlock, which then becomes a hip toss, tumble onto the back, hit the mat, and up for another variation.

At each stage of development, the goal is a kind of kinetic fluency, so that the wrestler—again like a dancer—comes to act and react reflexively, the knowledge in his body making it possible to move without consciously thinking. Ideally, as he incorporates the moves and variations into his body and psyche, he also comes to understand their logic, what the moves signify and how to shape sequences into a coherent whole. In other words, ideally, as his kinetic vocabulary expands, the wrestling student becomes capable of developing lines of action on the spot. He becomes adept, that is, at taking whatever moves his opponents make and integrating them into his own narrative, learning to walk the essentially unstable line between improvised and choreographed action. He learns to take what has been planned—the finish, a face or heel turn, a last-minute reversal, a chase through the audience—and embellish it in his own still-developing wrestler's language, so that the spectators can remain unsure as to which of his moves were planned and which accidents, which bits of violence were planned and controlled and which were accidental, actual, and out of control.

As a rule, the relative hierarchy of the game—who is inside, who is out—can be seen, literally, in the wrestlers' physical relationship to the ring itself. The more experienced wrestlers take priority in the ring, sometimes working out together for several hours before giving way to the novices, who generally spend that time off to the side working on mats on the floor. While the more experienced wrestlers spar with each other, playing roles—heel, face, tag-team partner, referee, spectator—with equal parts seriousness and cheerful mockery of themselves and each other, the youngsters are drilled in falling backwards and tumbling forwards, in basic holds and reversals, in lessons that can be as particular as how far apart their feet should be when stepping into the first lockup. At intervals, the wrestlers converge in the ring. The newer will watch the more experienced, and the more experienced will observe and coach the newer. All the wrestlers regularly bring in moves that they've seen at matches, or on television or on a video. Talking these moves through and attempting to replicate them is an intrinsic part of the training process. Someone may begin the workout saying, "I saw this great move on a video yesterday," and by the end of the day he will have not only assimilated the move into his repertoire, but, more important, embellished upon it and made it genuinely his own. Whether a task set by Johnny or something introduced by one of the other guys, the moves are worked through in slow motion, discussed, repeated, and elaborated upon so that what at first appears impossible and improvised, by the day's end can appear easy, smooth, and natural, as though anyone could pick it up in a quick try.

Practice matches essentially imitate the give-and-take and display of public performances, but with a kind of stop-and-start familiar to anyone who has attended a theatrical rehearsal. Two wrestlers will square off, with another often acting as referee and others acting as spectators. As they work with each other, they frequently exchange roles, tagging in and out, so that while they may stop and repeat moves, the practice itself can go on without an official ending for quite some time. Much like improvisational actors or dancers, they rely on kinetic memory to internalize and store combinations of moves. They run through patterns and variations, stopping sometimes on their own to get a move right, sometimes when another wrestler or Johnny offers a different way of responding to the opponent's moves. After an interruption, the sparring partners go back and repeat the previous sequence, incorporating and elaborating upon the suggested changes. They repeat sequences numerous times until they are satisfied that they have mastered the moves. Frequently, Johnny or another wrestler will step in to demonstrate a pattern or a variation, taking one side or the other of the exchange to make his point, so that what initially appear to be random movements seem, in the end, to have a clear pattern and logic.

The activity at Gleason's on 20 February 1993 is typical of the ongoing training process. When I arrive midday, Vito and Larry are working out in the ring. Johnny is off to the side with Mohammed and a new guy named Tom (not Tommy), on the mats generally reserved for the shadow boxers, their reflections distorted in the mylar mirrors. For over an hour after my arrival Johnny repeatedly alternates between demonstrating and critiquing their execution of two things: the distance and posture that should be maintained between men as they circle one another and the proper way to lunge to the standard first shoulder/elbow hold. Mohammed and Tom start their circle. Johnny stops them after two steps. He shows them again: They must keep about three feet apart. They start again. He stops them. "Don't bounce!" And he demonstrates a kind of tightly coiled, not bouncy, knees bent stance. He pushes at the backs of their knees, trying to give them the experience of the posture in their own bodies. They start again. He stops them. Their feet must stay in a precise relation to each other. He demonstrates, then physically shifts their feet. They start again. Not really satisfied, but in a gesture of resignation, he finally lets them progress to the lunge. They attempt to move into a perfectly balanced hold, opposite feet meeting every time. Circle, lunge, push back circle. Like an acting teacher or a ballet instructor, he watches, criticizes, explains, demonstrates, positions, watches.

A boxer walks by on his way to the locker room as Johnny is demonstrating. Johnny turns, grabs the other man, who responds defensively, reflexively stepping into the same hold that Johnny has been attempting to teach. After a moment, Johnny breaks the hold, slaps him (gently) on the shoulder, then laughs: "See. This guy knows what to do, and he ain't even been working on it." He tries to point out that it's common sense what he's trying to teach—nothing fancy, just what any man might do in a fight. They go back to their drill. When he leaves them for a minute to take a phone call in the main office, they keep at it for a while, with Mohammed taking the role of coach: explaining, demonstrating, positioning, and correcting Tom. After a moment or two Mohammed looks to see that Johnny isn't returning, then launches into a lesson of his own. Holding, turning, stepping behind Tom into the dominant position, attempting to throw him, Mohammed tries to explain both the physics and the psychology of the moves in his own words.

When Johnny returns, he stops Mohammed and takes them both into the ring, where he corrects their movements, from counterclockwise, which is awkward and destabilizing, to clockwise, which is fluid and controlled. As they continue, Johnny wanders in and out of focus, stopping and correcting the more experienced wrestlers on several occasions, and chatting with the boxers and wrestlers as they cross the area in transit to the locker room. Standing between Johnny and the ring, I attempt

Johnny teaches the hip toss to a new wrestler with Mohammed's help
(pages 77 and 78).

to observe and learn as much as possible myself. Indeed, when Johnny repeats something for what feels like the hundredth time, I experience a vivid moment of hubris, think for a fraction of a second: "Hell, even I could do that!" The moment quickly passes.

As the day winds down, Johnny stands with Larry outside the ring, watching and chatting. Vito takes on Nicky Cone of the Rhinos for a while, then tries to get Mohammed into the ring with him. Mohammed is understandably wary of Vito. Skeptical of Vito's intentions, Moham- med dodges his challenges with as much grace as he can muster and heads to the locker room. Vito jeers at him as he leaves, then strolls over to me for a bit of conversation about his own initiation process. Johnny offers me a ride back into the City, which I accept, and the day ends with a bit of inconsequential conversation in the car.

Thus, much of the wrestlers' training appears to occur on several levels at once, with each wrestler in turn reinforcing his own most recently acquired skills—whether in tumbling or in respect—by turning around to teach them to someone else. For the most part these intrafraternal lessons are more acts of generosity, themselves a sign of respect and a way of developing the bonds between the men, than they are a ritual

Mohammed takes over the lesson (pages 79, 80, and 81).

hazing per se. While violence is never far from the surface, and a lesson is always also a test, the urgency for the wrestlers is to create peers with whom they can work effectively and safely. The point is simple from their perspective: they have to know that the guy they're facing in the ring—whether in a workout or in performance—knows what he's doing, that he shares their understanding of the protocols of reciprocity and exchange, and at the very least that he won't hurt them without meaning to.

These basic principles are at stake a few weeks later (17 July 1993), when a new wrestler named Tony becomes the center of attention in the ring for a lengthy lesson from a wrestler I know as "the Romanian Warrior." A model and actor of sorts, Tony clearly has come to the ring with a background in bodybuilding: very muscular, bleached and blond, in a shiny new black unitard, who preens as though an invisible mirror held by a beautiful admiring woman follows him. He is destined to last only a few weeks, even though the other wrestlers suppress their obvious exasperation and treat him with remarkable patience, it seems. The Romanian attempts to teach Tony a body slam: how to take it, how to do it. The atmosphere in the gym grows increasingly strained as Tony repeatedly fails to get it. Tony keeps forgetting while in motion that being lifted is not simply work for the other guy. He can't seem to remember to plant his hand properly on the other man's thigh and to swing himself into the air, leaving the Romanian to lift and carry his 250 or so muscular pounds unaided. When he's throwing, he doesn't turn his body fully around, so that the Romanian keeps having to twist himself in order to avoid being injured when he hits the mat. The strain on the Romanian is evident, and he is increasingly worried for his back, but he continues taking both sides of the exchange and explaining the moves step by step to Tony for what seems like an hour.

The others step in, taking turns first demonstrating with the Romanian and then taking his place with Tony, doing the moves in slow motion, explaining over and over again that the man who is lifted must work as hard or harder than the one doing the lifting and that the one who is lifting and slamming must be protective of the one being lifted and slammed. On the sidelines, Larry tells me that Tony poses a high level of danger to himself and the others if he fails to assimilate this basic lesson and its equivalents: "It takes a higher level of concentration to protect him and yourself" (interview 1993). After Tony struts off to the showers, they tell me that they might not have been so nice if he didn't still owe Johnny money—another example of the wrestlers' communal ethics in practice.

Integrated into the wrestlers' training at all times are concepts, vocabularies, and ethics that extend well beyond the simply physical. Of these, what distinguishes the practice of wrestling from that of other sports are the lessons in making the performance engaging for the audience. Without the expressive logic of the wrestling event—the shaping of narratives within and around the performance, the deliberate pacing of action, the effort to make certain gestures visible while concealing others, and most of all the explicit incorporation of the audience into the performance— the spectacle of violence in professional wrestling would be more like boxing, in which from where I sit contests often appear brief and unspectacular indeed, simply that of two guys hitting each other until one falls to the mat for a very long time. What Johnny teaches, what the more experienced wrestlers come to reiterate, is how to stage a fight with force and conviction *for* and *with* an audience. Beyond learning *how to* wrestle, that is, Johnny's students must learn to *perform as* wrestlers. Beyond being violent, they must learn to display their violence and themselves appropriately. Above all, beyond learning strategies for winning a contest, they must also learn how to win an audience, how to convert spectators into fans.

A new wrestler's first lessons in performance are typically in maintaining the appearance of reality in the physical action while at the same time organizing and amplifying gestures and expressions so that the spectators can easily read and respond to the match as it unfolds. Sometimes Johnny rebukes a wrestler for overreacting to an obviously slight blow: "Who's gonna believe you if the guy didn't even connect?" He imitates the wrestler's overacting in an even more exaggerated cartoonish display in order to get his point across. Conversely, he often admonishes a wrestler who seems to be striving to look tough by appearing to be impervious to his opponent's blows: "You gotta sell the pain." And to a wrestler who repeatedly ignores the menacing of another: "You gotta do a dance and a song when he comes at you."

The lessons in theatricality and showmanship are thus as emphatic and precise as the lessons in the moves. While enforcing a kind of heightened verisimilitude, Johnny also constantly reiterates the importance of colluding both with the other wrestler and with the audience. Indeed, his lessons most often emphasize keeping the tension tautly triangulated among wrestler, opponent, and audience: "how to create the friction between you and the audience and the guy and everything" (interview 1989). It is as much about the wrestler's psychological placement relative to the audience as it is about the physical distance he keeps from his opponents, Johnny says, demonstrating ways of focusing the eyes on the front row in order to let the energy of the confrontation carry on to the spectators in the other rows. He often stops two wrestlers who seem to be working with impressive physical fluency to tell them that an uninterrupted flow of blows and throws quickly gets boring to watch. He reminds them to sell their moves to the spectators. "You gotta want the audience to want you to get him," he will tell one technically correct wrestler as he shows him how to open his actions visually and energetically to the audience. Menacing another wrestler, Johnny stops and holds him at arm's length, draws his fist back, and turns to look at me as he asks: "What should I do?" When I respond with "Kill him!" he might actually complete the gesture, hit and throw the young wrestler to the floor, or, playing against me as a heel, he might drop the guy and come over and argue with me.

Johnny's strategies for opening the performance to the audience often converge with strategies for varying the pace of the match as well as to give combatants time to figure their next moves. Stepping in to take one side of an exchange he demonstrates how to break a hold and strut away from the opponent toward the audience. Not only does this fundamental strategy allow the wrestlers to invite verbal and gestural exchanges with spectators, it offers the other guy the opportunity to ambush him, ideally provoking spectators to get actively involved either in warning a good guy or in colluding against a bad guy. Such strategies serve multiple purposes in a match, Johnny tells the wrestlers. To hold a punch, to break a hold, to shift from an attack, to stop and face the audience disrupts the status quo, revitalizes the action, and gives the wrestling event an explicit, dramatic shape that engages the audience in an unfolding narrative of violence as well as in its immediate expression.

As the wrestlers become more experienced, they internalize the presence of the audience, so that the rhythm of holding and opening, looking and demanding to be looked at is fully incorporated into their practice. In particular, I see Mohammed's "presence" in the ring grow more and more vivid. Watching him as he works out with newer wrestlers, the distance he has traveled is immediately apparent and the difference is acute. He is, simply, easier and more engaging to watch. His increasing physical control gives him the freedom to punctuate the moves with a look to the audience and to position himself so that he can make visible and sell the moves most effectively. But he also takes the floor with more confidence and force than would have been imaginable in his early weeks.

It becomes obvious, too, that at least a portion of my sense of being included in the workout as one of the guys is, in all likelihood, owing to the way in which they use me as a point on which to focus as they practice working the audience. I often feel the energy in the ring shift toward me the moment I plant myself in the corner. It is not simply a visceral sensation of their coming to awareness of my presence. The wrestlers literally begin to perform for and with me. The Mexican Wrestlers invariably begin to point all of their work at me, holding and looking at me for my applause and/or my camera. And at one workout in particular, I note that Larry and Vito begin by simply sparring with each other, but their workout becomes increasingly performative as they push each other between play and real violence, posture at and issue challenges to me as well as for each other. Vito pats himself on the back and insults me along with other, imagined spectators at all sides of the ring. Larry ends up on his knees, begging for mercy, looking from side to side to see if his imaginary audience is onto his perfidy. Even when alone in the ring, Larry works an imaginary audience, and when faced with a video camera and microphone, instantly spiels a whole scenario: spouting hatred against Mexicans, in particular the one holding the camera—"all those greasy wetbacks . . . who don't even speak Spanish well"—and challenging Johnny to fight, claiming that he will finish the job that his father "Jack Brisco" started in 1973 when he took Johnny Rodz apart at Madison Square Garden.

Above all, wrestlers learn that generating heat is as much about the shaping of action through interaction as it is about reciting the verbal and gestural clichés that superficially mark the wrestling event. It is not enough to wave the American flag or to shout (in Brooklyn) "Brooklyn sucks!" A kind of causality must be sustained. One action must lead logically to the next. At the same time, the match must contain an element of unpredictability. As Larry once reminded me, wrestling fans

Larry with Tommy sells the move to the "audience."

are quickly bored by the status quo, and, if one guy is just pounding another—no matter how tough he may appear as a result—the audience will simply get restless and turn off. He cites, as an example, his heel turn at the Gleason's show (22 April 1989). When he changed his plan, took the tag team trophy from his partner and handed it to the bad guys, both his partner's confused rage and the negative heat he generated from the fans were genuine. The best way to generate heat, then, is to exploit the conventions of wrestling, to work through the logic of the game in active nonverbal ways, playing with and against spectator expectations. The best point from which to orient logical lines of action is from the conventions of characterization, in particular from the ways in which the face or the heel traditionally behave in various circumstances.

This was the lesson that Larry was offering to Tommy and Chris on 25 June 1994, just before the violence erupted: a face displays pain differently than a heel when bodyslammed to the mat. Larry demonstrated. A face struggles against the pain. He may hold his back as a sign of injury but will press forward and challenge the heel to hit him while he's down. He makes his fortitude and determination all the more visible for being

Larry with Chris: "What should I do?"

injured. In contrast—again Larry demonstrated—a heel either crumbles with the pain, which may or may not be pretended, and retreats, or (more commonly) uses it to gain an advantage. Holding his back as a sign of injury, he will plead with the face to take pity on him all the while preparing to repay the face's generosity with a surprise attack. He makes his corruption and cowardice all the more visible for being injured. Mohammed and a few of the others watched from ringside, playing spectator along with me as the three men in the ring took turns role-playing and coaching each other. At every interval, they reminded each other to turn their faces to the audience, to find nonverbal ways to indicate what's going on without looking too fake.

It is not surprising, in retrospect, that when Larry exploded, he continued to talk to us, to demand our agreement that his attack on Tommy and Chris was justified, and to look to us from his dominant position as if to say, "See how easy it is for me. I must be right." He had gone from demonstrating ways of making spectators take sides for or against him in performance to demanding that we take his side regardless. The habit of engaging the audience is so ingrained that even when the sparring turns to actual violence, the performance of violence continues.

Chris begs for help from the "audience" as Larry puts on the pressure.

Like many performers in other entertainment industries, wrestlers create their characters by capitalizing on personal idiosyncrasies, an ethnic identity, or an attitude, and by developing them in relation to each other and an audience according to the rules of the game and the sensibilities of their community. The characters they become are, in the end, an amalgam between their individual identities and cultural stereotypes, developed as much in relation to each other and to the spectators as they are from preexisting options. Sometimes the choices are obvious: Vito's Von Kraut persona fits his physical stature and aggressive demeanor quite seamlessly, and it is hard to imagine him as a face. As someone with a claim to Native American heritage, almost always heroes in the current culture, Adolfo was wise (with Johnny's help) to develop himself as the image of a virtuous Indian, Little White Wolf. Sometimes the choices are apparently arbitrary, and the audience may not always go along with the plan: During the time I spent at Gleason's, Johnny changed the name of one young wrestler from "Diesel" to "Curly Man Don." But the audience at the next match (22 April 1989) paid no heed to this change, persistently chanting "Die-sel! Die-sel! Die-sel!" After trying a number of other variations on the wrestler's name, Johnny appeared to settle (at least for the December match) on "Diesel Don." Obviously, the more proficient a player becomes, the more fluid his public identity may be. Larry is very proud of his versatility, that he can swing from babyface to heel, in part simply by looking dumb and innocent, then acting smart and not-so-innocent, turning from buddy to bully in a flash (interview 1993).

According to Johnny, a wrestler's status as face or heel is largely determined by the audience's attitude toward him: "The promoters are out there watching the people watching the wrestlers. So they figure, 'Hey, this guy here, maybe he should be a little rougher' or maybe he starts pushing the guy into a position where the guy has to go over there and do a little more for the promoter's sake [like give an attitude]. Or maybe, 'I'll give you some money if you go over and yell at a couple of people' " (interview 1989). The basic rules of behavior are obvious: cheat, boast, insult the spectators, and act the coward if you're a heel; nearly succumb, then allow audience claps and cheers to lift you to victory if you're a face. Although wrestlers say that some guys simply come off as "bad," others as "good"—no matter what they actually do inside or out of the ring— and that very few can actually sustain a reversal for long, they all practice playing both types when they spar. In fact, many will switch sides opportunistically throughout their careers, as it appears to their advantage with promoters and audiences.

In developing and transforming their public personae, professional wrestlers always appear to be revealing, uncovering aspects of themselves formerly less visible to others. Indeed, the professional wrestler learns to make himself and his actions at once translucent and opaque. He must learn to control his moves and make them fluid so that they are visible and convincing to the audience. At the same time, he must also learn to mask his points of agreement with his opponent. He must develop a persona that is immediately, nonverbally resonant with the audience, becoming fluent in signaling his orientation as a face or heel and in reading and reacting to the audience's response, all the while wrestling and moving the match forward in a realistic way. He must learn to open his violence to the audience, to freeze-frame his punches and his tosses so that the audience has room to respond. And he must learn to shape the match on his feet, working within the conventions of the game, pacing the match from its slow start to the frenetic climactic exchange that, ideally, brings the spectators to their feet.

The wrestler's lessons are contradictory, the competing demands of the individual and the game in order to construct the match almost impossible to reconcile. At the same time that the wrestler learns to make his actions visible, he also must learn to mask his performance strategies. In sharing one level of his process—"What should I do?"—with the audience, the infrastructure of his real calculations—how can I get the audience really worked up?—must be made to disappear. While he works to "put himself over," to make himself stand out to audiences and promoters, he must also work in collusion with other wrestlers to create the spectacle, to put the other guy over. That is, he must learn to work with, while to the fans he appears to work against, the other man in the ring. Or, more precisely, he must learn to work with the other wrestler to give a show, while at the same time competing with that other wrestler for the audience's and the promoter's attention, to upstage while staging.

To this end, the pause before striking his opponent not only invites the audience in, it gives the opponent a moment to prepare to take the hit. Playing unconscious on the mat gives the wrestler breathing and thinking room. By not leaping to his feet as the referee counts him out, but struggling at the last moment, he plays on the audience's expectations as he figures out what he wants to do next. Strutting and jeering the audience at ringside gives the opponent a chance to attack. Arguing with the referee gives a tag-team partner room to wreak havoc outside the ring. It is in this way that wrestlers learn to work together to create opportunities for give-and-take, for the spectacular exchanges and displays of athletic virtuosity and theatrical audacity that mark the best of professional wrestling.

With its repetitions and humiliations, its tedium and periods of play, the process of training as a professional wrestler is designed to effect the transference of knowledge about wrestling from abstraction to action, from the realm of the imagination to that of the body, from the idea(l) of wrestling and the self as a wrestler to the work of practice and performance. The newcomer takes a beating at all levels, body and ego. He is forced to recognize that what looks easy from the sidelines is not, and that to be able to act a role while performing the moves—to walk the walk while talking the talk—requires discipline and determination through a long awkward, unrewarding period. To master the simplest moves, it seems, he must submit to repeated instructions, demonstrations, and hands-on placement of every part of his body.

A new professional wrestler may think he knows the important thing—that the matches are fixed and, consequently, that the emphasis is on displayed rather than actual violence—but he will not know what that means in actuality until he is forced to pull his own punches and give over a match to a wrestler who is higher up the ladder. He can only learn how to be on top by being, at least for a time, on the bottom. He cannot expect to play the winner unless he is well prepared to play the loser. Ultimately, to learn to look powerful and violent while protecting his opponent from injury he must experience what it is to have "his face pushed to the mat." The lesson is not abstract or intellectual. It must be experienced, generally more than once, for the wrestler to begin to come into his own, as the more experienced wrestlers at Gleason's have. He must learn to respect himself while respecting others. He must learn to display hostility and to act violently toward another man without actually damaging him. He must surrender his aggression, his competitiveness, his desire for victory, and his fear of humiliation to the demands of the promoter, the performance, and the game. If he refuses to play by the rules, whether in workouts or in matches, he runs the risk of vociferous derision at best and a serious beating at worst. For most, the lesson in respect is learned by testing the limits and tasting the consequences, not by talking or thinking about it or by figuring it out. Those who survive become real professional wrestlers, regardless of their visibility to outsiders.

But the humiliations of the first weeks have their compensations. As they learn to submit, paradoxically, wrestlers are also given seductive samples of empowerment. Within days of taking their first falls, Johnny deliberately asks newcomers to correct those even newer, to goad them through drills and to demonstrate moves learned sometimes just days before. Each participant is thus fully activated both as learner and teacher in the course of the day's workout. Beyond the obvious economies of such a strategy (not solely dependent upon Johnny's attention, each student gets far more bang for his buck) and the pedagogical advantages (every lesson is reinforced for the wrestler who turns to teach it to another) the students are made to feel their progress from neophyte to expert actively. That is, the student's rapid shift from learner to teacher is marked by his movement toward insider status, a sense of being a part of an exclusive masculine community, by taking partial responsibility for bringing another man inside. He gains respect as he learned to give it, by expecting it and, when necessary, extracting it forcefully from the new guy, the one who just walked in the door.

Watching Larry with Tommy, I remember other similar confrontations at Gleason's, including one with José more than a year before (17 April 1993). Many lessons occur simultaneously, with the line between teaching another man the rules of the game and teaching him how to be with other men impossibly blurred. José was one of the youngest and the slowest of the trainees—more needing of the fathering that Johnny offers and the stability of the wrestling community than in line for a career. Larry dominated José even more easily than he did Tommy, climbing over the younger man, working through holds and pressure points, twisting arms and legs. Half-mocking and half-guiding, Larry pushed him around the ring as the others egged both men on. At each hold, Larry froze and momentarily caught my eye, spotting me as "audience" while José alternately scrambled to escape and displayed the bravado that had gotten him into this position in the first place. José's discomfort as Larry pushed him around and Vito heckled him from the side was, at the time, yet another reminder of the complex interaction between physical strength and intellectual savvy in professional wrestling as well as of the fine line between playing at violence and being violent. That José stopped going to the gym not long after this encounter is probably owing more to his limited attention span than to the struggle with Larry. That I never saw Tommy at the gym again may have been owing more to my own absences than his, but he certainly was missing from the workouts in the weeks that immediately followed. When I had the opportunity to ask Larry how angry he actually was with Tommy, his response was that he's not sure himself how "real" his violence is at such moments, that even in sparring with Johnny at times the line seems to have been crossed, with neither man really certain afterwards of what happened. The only thing he knows for certain, he told me, is that he was just teaching Tommy a necessary lesson.

Chapter Four

REAL MEN DON'T WEAR SHIRTS

Yes, I've got lust. But it's not for Elizabeth. I've got lust for
you, Macho Man.

—Hulk Hogan

Wrestling is like making love to a woman.

—Larry Brisco

What is a "real" man?

"Here he is coming now directly to ringside. The one and only, the original 'Toast of the Coast' . . . 'the Human Orchid' . . . Gorgeous George!"[1] The videotape of classic wrestling performances from the 1950s and 1960s shows the crowd jeering as a big, somewhat soft-looking man dressed in what might be recognized as full Liberace drag enters the ring. A sequined robe and artificially shaped blond curls top his wrestler's trunks and shoes: "The Hellenic look by Frank and Joseph of Hollywood," the announcer tells us. Complacently patting his coif, Gorgeous George adds: "With Grecian contours." In the opposing corner, Larry Moquin looks to be on the verge of imploding in his plain trunks and short dark hair. In contrast to Gorgeous George, who is, we are told, "powdered to perfection," Moquin epitomizes the brute. As the straight man, wrestling in earnest, he is repeatedly frustrated and increasingly flummoxed as Gorgeous George flaunts and taunts. The powdered one breaks the rules one minute and accuses Moquin of hair-pulling the next. He minces and primps and then, in flashes of athleticism, demonstrates astonishing wrestling prowess, although his victory in the end is ill-won as any heel's should be. As the referee designates Gorgeous George the winner, and Moquin protests vehemently, Gorgeous George himself appears more concerned with the proper draping of the "snood" of his floral "sweating robe"—"Oh brother!" exclaims the announcer—that is, until Moquin hits him over the head with the silver tray on which the robe was presented.

Gorgeous George was a heel with heat. His flaunting, taunting performances provoked loud, exuberant expressions of apparently homophobic antipathy in the audience. Morton and O'Brien cite "the prissy, marcelled villainous ring persona of Gorgeous George" as a prime example of the "star people loved to hate" (47). It is Gorgeous George, they tell us, whose performances worked the archetype of the "narcissistic brawler, proud of his own beauty and talents while condescending towards his foes. . . . [His] flashy tights and immaculately kept hair set a standard that has been followed by numerous wrestlers and by his most famous disciple, Muhammad Ali" (134). The performances of Gorgeous George also provide the beginning, and many times the end point, for much of the conventional wisdom about the performance of masculinity in professional wrestling. While Gorgeous George certainly displayed what a real man is not, under his feminine frippery, he always revealed himself to be a match for the brutes he opposed. His evident success in generating heat, his "pop" from the fans, appears to have been complex rather than simple, as much about identification as condemnation, as Clifton Jolley rhapsodizes in his PBS documentary *I Remember Gorgeous George*: "Most people thought he was ridiculous in those robes. But all I could see was that he was free to do and to act any way he wanted."

Try again. What is a "real" man?

Another star from the same period, and in the same video collection of vintage wrestling performances, Ricky Starr—"from Greenwich Village, weighing 201 pounds"—literally prances and dances into the ring to the cheers of the crowd.[2] He teases the ring announcer with a miniature pair of ballet slippers that match the pair on his feet before tossing them to the audience. Catching one of the slippers, the commentator speculates that he will "wind up marrying Ricky Starr now, because I caught the wreath," and he continues to point toward Starr's apparent femininity (read homosexuality) without much subtlety or respite throughout the match. He notes that "Ricky's letting his hair grow out . . . on his chest," and adds, "That's a lovely pair of trunks Ricky *almost* has on." Later he compares him to midget wrestlers, "except those midgets are a little taller." Novelist and essayist Angela Carter's admiration of Starr includes a description of watching him perform "a pirouette or two before getting down to business" ("Giant's Playtime" 228). Indeed, billed as an ex-ballet dancer formerly of the Ballet Russe de Monte Carlo, Ricky Starr dances more than he wrestles in the first part of his match against Karl von Hess. The commentator remarks: "They don't get much wrestling done here. But we sure have a lot of fun, don't we? . . . See, Starr's a good wrestler when he wants to be, when he cuts out the clowning. But who wants him to cut out the clowning?"

Starr's performance, especially his taunting of von Hess, is explicitly (homo)sexual. He wiggles his buttocks under the other wrestler's nose while pretending to straighten his shoe, performs a series of pelvic thrusts, and hops on and off von Hess's back, controlling his opponent with apparent ease and leading the commentator at one point to worry half-seriously about the network censors: "Mr. Starr is just loosening up. Nothing wrong with that. Wish he would loosen up out of camera, though. This is a family network, you know." As Starr continues, the commentator informs us that Starr was taught his moves by an old (male) burlesque star who went by the name of "Toots" and that: "This program [is] sponsored by bumps and grinds incorporated." Von Hess snarls and plays it as straight as a villain can under the circumstances. Clearly the loser in the fan sweepstakes as well as the match, he is finally defeated by Ricky Starr's rapid and proficient series of drop kicks. In a coda to the match, von Hess gets into a slugfest with the referee, which ends when Starr intervenes on the ref's behalf, taking a hit himself in the process.

From the outside, professional wrestling is perhaps most transgressive for the way in which it puts the "cute" in the ring with the "brute." Its presentations of the "not-so-real," "not-so-manly" man are vividly marked by the conventional clichés of homosexual performance: he dances (read minces) and teases, even offers himself to other men. In performance Ricky Starr, like Gorgeous George, appears to have violated all the protocols of masculine, heterosexual propriety. His performance can be recognized as a kind of camp—a male "burlesque" as the commentator terms it—and yet its transgressions seem to be accepted and even celebrated by its audience. Far from being reviled by the presumably straight, lower- and working-class audience of the fifties and sixties, this blithe spirit was a fan favorite, earning cheers for his fancy footwork in the ring. His status as a not-so-manly hero who nonetheless proves his machismo in action is not accidentally generated nor is it solely self-created. Rather it appears to be constructed both by the commentator, whose playful contributions seem in direct contrast to the drier commentary that accompanies Gorgeous George's match against Larry Moquin, and by the other players, who give Starr the opportunity to "rescue" the referee after the match has officially ended.

Although even more "cute" than Gorgeous George, Starr likewise proves himself equal to the brute he opposes, the epitome of what Angela Carter terms "a man who is working at playing" (228) or perhaps more accurately, a man who is playing at working. He dominates the match with a demonstration of wrestling skill and savvy that goes well beyond flummoxing von Hess with his feminine wiles. Admittedly, the audience's (and the commentator's) appreciation of Starr's cliché homosexual display may be no less rooted in heterosexism if not homophobia. It is possible that at best their laughter is only transiently transgressive, perhaps celebrating a kind of carnivalesque outing, a trip to the homosexual freak show on terms Moe Meyer in *The Politics and Poetics of Camp* recognizes as highly ambivalent when he remarks: "The bourgeois subject of camp *celebrates* the invisibility of the queer, rejoices in the act of appropriation, and, in effect, derives *pleasure* from the erasure of the queer" (15). But it is also clear that in the ethos and aesthetics of professional wrestling the "not-so-manly" man always carries the potential to reveal and revel in his "real" manliness.

Again. What is a "real" man?

WrestleMania IX (4 April 1993) at Caesar's Palace in Las Vegas. Music shimmers as do the four showgirls in gold lamé bikinis and high heels who escort "the Narcissist" Lex Luger, his body cloaked in a silver and lavender lamé cape, to the open-air ring. At ringside, commentating with Randy Savage, Bobby "the Brain" Heenan is comparing Lex Luger to a Greek god, but breaks off as the camera shows a rear view of the women climbing the stairs to the ring: "Ooooh baby!" exclaims Savage. Heenan adds "Oh yeah!" and boasts that the one on the end has an eye for him.

The showgirls pose opposite Luger as he takes a stroll around the ring. They then lift four shieldlike mirrors, which erupt in orgasmic fireworks as Luger removes his cloak revealing a superbly developed bodybuilder's body in white and lavender briefs. He alternately displays his body and admires himself in the mirrors and poses for the audience, flexing his pecs and wiggling his hips. The girls set the mirrors on the mat and leave Luger alone in the ring. On their way out they pass Mr. Perfect (Curt Hennig), a newly turned face, whose former gimmick was, like Luger's, located in his narcissism. Perfect glances appreciatively at the one who taps his cheek but immediately gives his smiling attention over to the cheering fans and appears to be concentrating on the match ahead. Dressed in a neon green Lycra singlet, snapping gum and flipping a white handtowel, he leaps to the ring and briefly encourages the fans before squaring off with Luger.

With their unnaturally blond ringlets, suntanned bodies, and apparent eagerness to injure each other, the men appear as reflections of one another. But they are not quite equal, and it is not a fair fight. Luger repeatedly cheats and pleads to avoid losing, and he wins in the end because of the referee's failure to see that Perfect is caught in the ropes. Not content with the victory itself, Luger knocks Perfect unconscious and performs another set of bodybuilder poses with his foot planted on the other man's chest before strutting away. Perfect comes to and follows Luger outside the arena, but his attempt to extract justice, to reclaim his manhood by fighting Luger outside the ring—man-to-man, "for real" instead of "for performance"—is thwarted by Shawn Michaels, another WWF heel who, making ample use of the large packing boxes and garbage cans conveniently stacked nearby, beats him unconscious once again.

In professional wrestling's mirrored funhouse, the only thing that is certain is that the "not-so-real" man is not a woman. The showgirls are presented to the live and pay-per-viewer in order to provide, literally, a mirror to the Narcissist. In the appearance of the showgirls, what Lex Luger *is*—someone who, like a woman, develops and displays his body as an object for others to admire—as well as what he *is not*—a woman—is made visible. The women's display of perfectly tanned and toned flesh is superseded and displaced by his own. It is a masterful introduction, especially in the way it works toward capturing and holding the audience's gaze. All eyes are on Luger, even his own. No matter where the audience begins its looking, its "look" is always directed toward Luger.

Not only does he explicitly demand our attention by posing for us, the showgirls also look at and admire him, while he looks at and admires himself.

Yet the more important reflection is that provided by Mr. Perfect. The difference between the showgirls and Luger is obvious and essential, located first and foremost in the display of the male and female bodies. The difference between Luger and Perfect is not. They are both, essentially, "cute brutes." Their bodies are more alike than different. In fact, ironically, at this match Perfect was completing a turn from a heel whose gimmick was, in part, his aggressive narcissism. Who is the manly man and who is the not-so-manly man must be revealed in action, in their performances. Luger's display of feminine vanity is marked as superficial by the presence of "real" women. The true means by which his masculinity is defined and his manliness tested is in action against a man who is very nearly his double, whom he is as much like as unlike.

A year later, Luger has turned face and fights Yokozuna, an apparently invincible Japanese monster (really a Samoan from San Diego, if hardcore fan information is to be believed), for the World Championship belt at *WrestleMania X* in Madison Square Garden (20 March 1994). As a coda to the perfidy of *WrestleMania IX*, Mr. Perfect appears as the guest referee, turns heel, and throws the match to Yokozuna, leaving both Luger and the audience outraged. But the highlight of *WrestleMania X* is a "ladder match" for the Intercontinental Championship between Razor Ramon ("the Bad Guy") and Shawn Michaels ("the Heartbreak Kid"). The two men emerge one at a time from the gate in a haze of smoke and light and strut to the ring accompanied by pounding music. Both men are visibly hardbodied, toned, and tanned. Both have hair that is short on top and falls in ringlets to their shoulders. Shawn Michaels wears red chaps over his long white Lycra pants, which have "Heartbreak Kid" scripted on his buttocks and broken hearts in red; his chest, waist, and ears are heavily weighted with silver chains and pendants. He enters with his black-leather-clad "bodyguard" Diesel, who watches as Michaels bumps and grinds to the crowd's jeers, and who is dismissed when the match begins. Razor Ramon enters alone, "oozing machismo." He is wearing black briefs with a green razor emblazoned across the buttocks and draped in gold chains as well as carrying his trademark toothpicks—one in his mouth, the other (a spare?) behind his ear. The referee is removed to ringside: this is a no-rules, no-ref match in which the two men are expected to prove themselves by fighting to the bitter end. They strip their accessories, Ramon warning the ring boy with a flick of his toothpick to be careful of the gold, and get down to wrestling.

The ladder match between Shawn Michaels and Razor Ramon is a hard-core fan's dream. The men are apparently evenly matched, displaying a high degree of athletic and performative prowess as they work each other over. When the aluminum ladder enters the ring, it is used both as a weapon and as an instrument for prolonging the suspense. Michaels, in particular, climbs multiple times to its top and from there slams himself and the ladder against Ramon's body. Ramon also uses the ladder to hit Michaels, and both men repeatedly take turns exposing themselves to danger by climbing almost to the top as the other knocks him down. The match climaxes when Ramon reaches the belts just as Michaels swings the ladder out from under him. Ramon crashes to the mat, the victor and new Intercontinental Champion. The arena twinkles with thousands of camera flashes, and the crowd roars its triumph as the visibly exhausted victor raises the championship belt over his head.

What is the difference between Michaels and Ramon? It seems that, in the end, only the question of who wins and how distinguishes one manly man from the other.[3] Both wrestlers swagger, strut and show, boast and bully. Both get down to all-out wrestling, hitting and being hit, climbing and falling, apparently struggling to the limits of their endurance regardless of the wear and tear on their bodies.[4] The very ambiguity of the presentation of the differences between these two men *as* men ironically problematizes the signs by which men are to be recognized. Perhaps the "real" man in the end is the one who proves his masculinity by winning, and the not-so-real, not-so-manly man is the loser in an arena where masculinity is as contested as are belts and titles. What a wrestler risks in the wrestling performance is perhaps not so much injury, but emasculation.

What is a "real" man? In wrestling, as in life, the signs by which one can recognize a "real" man and the differences between men are not necessarily fully visible or stable. What is revealed in the mirror of the other man is their essential sameness. What differentiates and separates them is ultimately superficial, the difference between a flip of the hip and a flick of a toothpick. In the ring, *any* man can be a "real" man, no matter how superficially feminine or lacking in virtue. A "real" man may fool around when the opportunity presents itself, but he also will struggle to prove himself to the bitter end, even if in the end he loses the contest and with it a bit of his machismo. There is, after all, always a new challenge to be issued, another chance to reclaim one's claim to the masculine ideal. Every professional wrestling event offers every man, whether performer or fan, a test of his manliness. The wrestler takes the opportunity to prove himself directly in action, while from the stands, the fan has the chance to see himself mirrored in the range of masculinities presented, to participate in judging the relative masculinity of other men, and to reassure himself of one certainty: at least he is not a woman.[5]

The conventional signs of femininity and masculinity are both medium and message in the wrestlers' closet, visibly encoded into everything from the wrestlers' names and costumes to their bodies and signature moves. To some degree, a professional wrestler is always in drag, always enacting a parody of masculinity at the same time that he epitomizes it. Professional wrestling is often accused of selling its audience—particularly the young pre- and just-adolescent men who are its most fervent fans and target consumers—a model of masculinity that is at once vulgar, violent, and sexually suspect in its sometimes lurid heterosexism and barely suppressed homoeroticism. Indeed the thriving business in wrestling videos of an explicitly homoerotic nature remains generally unacknowledged by and as such invisible within the dominant heterosexual culture.[6] With its extravagant displays of feathers and fights, professional wrestling does indeed appear to pit an antimasculine, or at least an ambivalently masculine, aesthetic and ethos against one that is hypermasculine. Its excessive male-body-centered performances confront and confound prohibitions limiting such displays to women, and as a result appear simultaneously to subvert and to legitimize the very idea(l) of the American man. Yet, despite its apparent transgressions—and even though women are always visible in the margins and in the audience—professional wrestling is always a performance by men, for men, about men. Both its ethos and its aesthetics are explicitly centered on the idea of masculinity as something at once essential and performed.

Professional wrestling's play of masculinity is profoundly carnivalesque as it affirms and mocks, celebrates and critiques prevailing definitions of what it is to be a "real" man in contemporary American culture. Because it is centered on, and always returns to, the display of male bodies and because the action is both a simulation and a parody of violence between men, the performance is always highly ambivalent and profoundly transgressive, at once hypervisible and hypermasculine. Michael Sorkin in "Simulations: Faking It" tells us: "Wrestlers are hypervisible: renown results from the combination of literal enormity (of muscle, of hairiness, of avoirdupois) with excessively schematic presentations of personality. Wrestlers never merely speak, they shout. Their selves are compounded of aggressiveness plus a single mediating component which allows the spectator to rapidly comprehend whether theirs is a force for good or ill" (164). They proclaim unyielding enmity, yet their apparently fierce blows rarely cause serious injury and seem, in the end, as mocking of themselves as their challenges are of each other. They flaunt their enlarged and excessively developed bodies in exaggerated costumes drawn from and elaborating upon cultural stereotypes: the Macho Latino, the Boy Toy, the Ghetto Blaster, the Native American, the Nature Boy, the Biker, the Surfer, the Dancer, the Trucker, the Preacher, the Professor, and so on. Often their names insinuate an exaggerated sexuality and imply sexual insults more appropriate to burlesque stage than to the sports arena: Gorgeous George, Rowdy Roddy Piper, Ravishing Rick Rude, Brutus Beefcake, Jake the Snake, and so on.

In his discussion of what he calls "carnival culture," James Twitchell recognizes the medievalism in wrestling's contemporary joust: "True, the knights and giants have been democratized and unionized. They no longer play the parts of princes-in-training and ersatz giants but are street-smart working men, bellowing braggarts, trend-setting macho fashion plates, and greedy capitalists—all images drawn from the day-to-day world of the audience" (226). Yet, as in the Middle Ages, in the wrestling world the surface of a character is all, yet it is not as it seems. A hero may reveal himself as a villain over time. An apparent "sissy" may indeed show his moral and physical strength under duress. Like Bakhtin's rogues, clowns, and fools, the wrestlers "create around themselves their own special little world," which is "connected with that highly specific, extremely important area of the square when the common people congregate" (*Dialogic Imagination* 159). The wrestlers are both real and not-real, in Bakhtin's words, "one cannot take them literally, because they are not what they seem. . . . Their existence is a reflection of some other's mode of being—and even then, not a direct reflection. They are life's maskers; their being coincides with their role, and outside this role they simply do not exist" (*Dialogic Imagination* 159).

From cute to brute, the types of man represented in the squared circle are, at first glance, extraordinarily diverse and by no means mutually exclusive or discrete. The flamboyant parodic femininity of a Gorgeous George or a Goldust intersects with the comic-book drag of an Undertaker or a Mountie or a Kamala or an Ultimate Warrior and collides with the rocker/outlaw machismo of a Randy Savage or a Shawn Michaels or a Rowdy Roddy Piper or a Razor Ramon, all of which doubles back and confronts itself more or less out of drag in the apparently earnest masculinity of a Larry Moquin, a Tatanka, a Hulk Hogan, or even a Vince McMahon. Superficially, it appears that the truth about men is that they are so antagonistically individuated that, while they idealize a brotherhood of man, in practice they cannot come within sixteen or eighteen feet of one another without coming to blows. Superficially, it appears that "real" men are American patriots who, when they fight for a title also fight for "all of America" as Lex Luger proclaimed in multiple interviews in the shadows of the Washington Monument and Mount Rushmore throughout 1994. Superficially, it appears that "real" men wear fewer sequins and less makeup than "not-so-real" men, and they tend not to worry about their hair so much.

But for all that wrestling displays the antagonism of difference, it also and more importantly affirms what it is these men have in common— that is, that they are men. What is at stake in the squared circle in each individual performance and what is sold to, as well as celebrated with, the audience is nothing less than an underlying idea(l) of a homogeneous community of men, whose differences are always understood to be superficial, a kind of drag overlay on an essential masculinity. As Angela Carter recognizes: "The 'mask' or persona of the wrestler bears no connection at all to his actual prowess" (228). That is, the proof of the man is not in his appearance, which he manipulates for his own and our pleasure. The proof of the man is in the force and skill he applies, whether he wins or loses, with and against other men. When Gorgeous George stops patting his hair and grapples with Larry Moquin, when Ricky Starr stops his pirouettes and drop-kicks Karl von Hess into a squirming mass on the floor, when Mr. Perfect pursues Luger out of the arena, when Shawn Michaels pulls himself from the floor in a last, futile attempt to prevent Razor Ramon's reach for the championship, what is made visible is nothing less than manliness itself, the will and spirit of a "real" man as it underlies and transcends both character and circumstances, latent (if not immediately apparent) in all men.

What is celebrated in the give-and-take of the match, in the appearance of loss and the retrieval of victory, is nothing more or less than manliness itself, the masculine idea(l). The action at the heart of the event is simple and predictable, as ritualized as Sunday Mass, as temporal and celebratory as Mardi Gras, and as much a rite of passage as a Bar Mitzvah or, perhaps more to the point, the primal masculinist rites envisioned by Robert Bly, in which "older men welcome the younger into the ancient, mythologized, instinctive male world" (*Iron John* 15). One after the other, men test their strength and wits against each other in a highly codified pattern of give-and-take, which requires a period of loss and humiliation regardless of outcome. Professional wrestling's spectacle of domination and submission offers its audiences a ritually circumscribed and performed test of manhood that is resolved in a climactic scene of reversal and recognition in which one man holds another (apparently disabled and as such at least temporarily emasculated) man, to the floor while he is judged the victor. This play is tragic if the hero loses unjustly, as when Mr. Perfect loses his match to Lex Luger at *WrestleMania IX* and again when Perfect causes Luger to lose his chance for the World Championship belt at *WrestleMania X*. Conversely, it is comic if he wins, as when Razor Ramon finally pulls the championship belts from the sky at *WrestleMania X*, taking the title of Intercontinental Champion from Shawn Michaels. What is at stake is more than the immediate loss or victory. The stability of the world order is embodied by one man at a time. When the "MegaPowers Explode" (*WrestleMania V*), the world is temporarily cast into disorder. When Hulk Hogan rises triumphant from his successful pinning of Randy Savage to place the World Championship belt on his waist, the world—or at least the fans—celebrates with him.

Henry Jenkins points to wrestling as a "Masculine Melodrama" in which live and televised performances externalize emotions, mapping them "onto the combatant's bodies and transforming their physical competition into a search for a moral order" (1). According to Jenkins, wrestling appropriates its performance structures both from the nineteenth-century theatrical tradition and from contemporary feminine versions of melodrama (including, of course, soap opera), in particular "its seriality, its focus on multiple characters and their relationship[s], its refusal of closure, [and] its appeal to viewer speculation and gossip" (4). The story told is indeed a contemporary morality play, in Jenkins's words again, "a story of justice perverted and restored, innocence misrecognized and recognized, strength used and abused" (12).

Professional wrestling thus conflates the idea(l) of justice with that of masculinity. The struggle for Justice against insult and suffering in wrestling is most often understood as a struggle to assert the masculine ideal against the constant threat of emasculation, with the wrestling event making visible a representative man's effort to stave off the encroachments of a civilized (read feminizing) modern life. Assumptions of a homogeneous lower working-class identification between the wrestlers and audience has led to a conventional reading of the wrestling event as the manifestation of a desire to see the world reduced into simple binaries of good and evil, just and unjust, manly and not-so-manly. Yet these assumptions are belied by the heterogeneity of wrestling's actual (as opposed to imagined) audience as well as by its constant turning on itself, its playful juxtapositioning of the apparently real with the obvious fake, of the superficially serious with obvious mockery. Wrestling's distinctions, its representations of virtue and vice, as well as of sissy and bully, are constantly slipping as it works to surprise and seduce the fans, "giving them what they want." Given wrestling's heavy reliance on the face or heel turn for dramatic weight, this masculine melodrama is more complex and contradictory than scholarly interpretations generally admit. Not only is Justice regularly denied to the virtuous, more important, the markers by which the Just identify themselves are not necessarily attached to masculinity or femininity, or to the social or antisocial per se. The "manly man" is no more likely to be virtuous in the end than is the "womanly man" likely to act the villain.

What professional wrestling offers over and over again for the spectators' consumption is an exaggeration of the continuum of masculine identifications available to men in contemporary American culture. Opposing each other are not simply representations of virtue and vice. Rather professional wrestling presents a range of positive and negative stereotypes of men whose relationship to each other, to the officials and other players, and to the spectators is constructed from and articulates a relationship to underlying assumptions of what real men are and do. Because these masculinities—from the flamboyantly feminine to the lumpen macho—may be positioned on either side of the morality line at any given time, what is always defined and placed at risk along with truth, justice, and the American way are shifting idea(l)s of manliness itself.

As in the medieval carnival that Bakhtin idealizes in *Rabelais and His World*, professional wrestling asserts an idea of communality alongside the rogue's "right to be 'other' in this world, the right not to make common cause with any single one of the existing categories that life makes available; none of these categories quite suits them, they see the underside and the falseness of every situation. Therefore they can exploit any position they choose, but only as a mask" (*Dialogic Imagination* 159). What the wrestlers celebrate is the freedom as men to create themselves anew with every match, to act the hero or the villain, the purist or the cheat, the manly or the not-so-manly man, at will. Even the performance of emasculation is ultimately simply that, a performance.

In the wrestling performance the distinctions between the "real" man and the "not-so-real" man may seem at first glance to be clear and obvious, as such explicitly aligned with the representation of virtue and vice, and staged in conventional terms that are easily recognized and evaluated by the spectators. The "real" man plays by the rules of the game, rules that ultimately reflect the social order itself, even as they are revealed to be flimsy guardians against rule-breaking. As he relies on the rules, so too he relies on himself, on his own strength and skill, as revealed by his exposed musculature and status as a "scientific" wrestler, rather than on managers or other associates. At the same time, he stands with and for the community of (manly) spectators. He not only welcomes its support, he directly depends upon its approbation for his success. In the narrative that contextualizes and authorizes his performance, the hero has usually worked hard for his shot at a title. When he is injured in the fight, he doesn't complain. He fights back through the pain and threat of humiliation, revealing his greatness most when he is at risk of losing all. For him and for the community he represents, a "real" man is one who stands up against gimmickry and perfidy, who takes a beating as well as being able to dish one out, who retrieves his victories from defeat by virtue (pun intended) of his greater will and his alignment with spectators.

As a "not-so-real" man, the heel inverts these values and positions himself in opposition to both the rules and the spectators. In contrast to the face, the heel generally displays more gimmickry and feminine frippery (including the occasional simpering or snarling woman on his arm), which are generally understood as smoke screens for his inadequacies as well as aids to cheating. Indeed, the conversion from face to heel is most often quickly recognizable by his acquisition of such markers. When injured he cringes with the pain and pleads for mercy from the face. If the face relents for a moment, the heel invariably takes advantage, revealing the fakery in his own performance. The heel is not content to rely on his strength or skill—even if these are in evidence and, as a face, he was known as a "scientific" wrestler. His victories depend mostly on the breakdown of order and the covert assistance of managers and other associates. Thus, while the face represents the real man, the heel is literally and visibly the cheat and the fake in the professional wrestling performance. Whereas the face is a kind of literal embodiment of the masculine ideal, the heel parodies, critiques, and ultimately exposes the fallacies of that ideal.

What the wrestlers' performance offers the audience is both recognition and license, in Bakhtinian terms:

> In the struggle against conventions, and against the inadequacy of all available life-slots to fit an authentic human being, these masks take on an extraordinary significance. They grant the right *not* to understand, the right to confuse, to tease, to hyperbolize life; the right to parody others while talking, the right not to be taken literally, not 'to be oneself'; the right to live a life in the chronotope of the entr'acte, the chronotope of theatrical space, the right to act life as a comedy and to treat others as actors, the right to rip off masks, the right to rage at others with a primeval (almost cultic) rage—and finally, the right to betray to the public a personal life, down to its most private and prurient little secrets. (*Dialogic Imagination* 163)

Despite—or indeed because of—wrestling's exaggeration and exploitation of cultural stereotypes, what the event celebrates is not a reiteration but rather an unleashing of social inhibitions on masculine and masculinist expression, from the hypermasculine to the apparently feminine. The event remains ambivalent, a carnival that—again in Bakhtinian terms—is simultaneously "gay, triumphant, and at the same time mocking, deriding. It asserts and denies, it buries and revives" (*Rabelais and His World* 12–13). The masculinity represented therein is likewise both idealized and mocked, disrespected and valorized. What is manly, in the end, is defined by each man as he looks in the mirror provided by other men. As it is essentialized, located in his body and continually elaborated upon in action, a man's masculine identity is not constrained by the social order. He can be whatever he chooses, as Clifton Jolley remembers of his adolescent delight at the extravagance of Gorgeous George's performance, "free to do and act any way he wanted."

Whether in the give and take of the workout or in the reversals of the performance, what wrestlers enact and enforce is a recognition of their shared masculinity, their essential man-ness. To watch Gorgeous George first flaunting his sequins and curls and then erupting with a flash sequence of expertly executed moves against his opponent is to witness a performance that threatens to destabilize an audience's assumptions about what real men are and what they do. But as it invites the audience's expressions of antagonism, it also acknowledges and affirms his performance as transgressive, implicitly recasting the masculine norm back to his opponent. Further, as he reveals his own not inconsiderable skill, he drops his drag, at least for the moment, and aligns himself with the masculine norm. He can play the man too, he implies, if and when he chooses.

Instead of offering fans a presentation of masculinity that is singular and conservative, the professional wrestling performance presents two or more contradictory possibilities poised against and coexisting with each other. Masculinity is both a choice and an essence, simultaneously an option and an imperative. While the professional wrestling performance always presents a version of masculinity that is sanctioned by the dominant culture, its presentation of alternative masculinities as concurrent proposes a community of men that is inclusive of a wide range of identities and behaviors, as such heterogeneous rather than homogeneous. Rather than prescribing limitations to masculine behavior, professional wrestling recognizes the official version at the same time that it acknowledges and, it might be argued, even encourages the unleashing of masculine expressivity in all forms. It is no wonder, then, that professional wrestling is remembered so fondly by so many men as a key part of their adolescent transition into adult masculinity and sexuality, a step toward understanding the self as a man among other men.

Just as Gleason's wrestlers are distinguished from the solitary or paired boxers in the way they gather as a group in the ring, the idea(l) of the individual man, the hero who steps forward alone to face another man, is carefully balanced by and against the idea(l) of the community of men.

Rubio and Frankie's workout shows the sensuality of Lucha Libre.

Underlying, and underlined by, the performance, and as such essential to the culture of the ring, are the points of agreement between the wrestlers, between the wrestlers and other players, and between the wrestlers and spectators, without which the wrestling event would be meaningless and perhaps impossible. As the preceding chapter demonstrates, the focus in training is as much on assimilating the game's fraternal codes as it is on learning to display and act upon antagonism between men. A wrestler learns "respect" for himself, for his peers, and for the game and in the process comes to act like a man, to expect to be treated as such by other men, and to punish or be punished for any transgressions thereof. As Larry Brisco once told me: "You've gotta protect yourself and if a guy tries to give you a problem, you give him a problem back. He has to respect you. Sometimes a guy will play with you just to see how much he can get away with and you just have to stop him on the road" (interview 1989).

"Real" professional wrestlers must often give ground as well as hold it. They must step back from a fight as well as into it, and as a result must learn and practice other, less conventional ways of expressing their masculinity in performance. Otherwise there is no performance, only a fight. As Larry told me recently when I reminded him of his confrontation with Tommy at Gleason's: "The whole thing is to get the point across somehow that shooting is pointless. If the matches were real [that is, if the point was simply to hurt the opponent], not only would we be carried out on stretchers, but nobody would care to watch" (DeGaris, e-mail correspondence 26 January 1997). The lesson in respect is not the end point but rather the stepping-stone toward the trust that is imperative in a sport that displays without necessarily actualizing violence between men, that offers up repeated images of embraces between men rather than the hit and break of most other sports—the "real" violence of boxing or football, for example.

Professional wrestling's status as a suspect, transgressive sport is intimately tied to amateur wrestling's exceptionally high level of extended physical contact, that is, to the idea of "grappling" itself. DeGaris notes in his discussion of "Professional Wrestling's Commercial Exploitation of Homophobia": "Wrestlers, both amateur and professional are often questioned about engaging in close physical contact with members of the same sex, especially while barely clothed." And he recalls that as a high school and collegiate wrestler his own response was "It's not gay, it's kicking ass" (3). As was evident in the workouts at Gleason's, the lesson in developing and managing a wrestler's body always implicitly included learning how to channel and/or deny sexual as well as violent impulses. Paradoxically, as the wrestlers move from the solitary drills of the early days to holding and throwing each other, they also learn to touch without touching, to be touched without being touched.

Wrestling is thus poised at what Kenneth Dutton in his discussion of the male body beautiful calls the point of "hesitation between admiration and attraction" (66). Both the practice and the performance of professional wrestling may be viewed as simultaneously homophobic and homoerotic, or as DeGaris terms it "homosensual" (e-mail correspondence 23 December 1996).[7] The prohibition against sexualizing the contact between men is unspoken but nonetheless emphatic: "If I give you my body, you'd better respect it" (DeGaris, e-mail correspondence 24 December 1996). As with other lessons in respect, the line between acceptable and unacceptable behavior is unmarked and ambiguous, contingent upon context, as much about learning how to be with other men as it is about learning how to be a particular kind of man. Because the line between managing and expressing desire is not solid, but rather shifting and unclear, the danger of crossing it and the threat of punishment (humiliation and/or physical injury) remain present as an undercurrent of anxiety, which as it is unresolved contributes to the visceral experience of the workout and the performance. Never explicitly acknowledged as erotic by wrestlers or by watchers, although sometimes played with by commentators, this tension is nonetheless intrinsic to wrestling's attraction. Professional wrestling thus offers participants the actual or vicarious pleasures of participating in physical contact between men in a sanctioned arena while at the same time inhibiting or denying the possibility that those pleasures might be sexual.

In the wrestling performance, the idealization of respect and trust that underlies the game surfaces in the moments when one man turns to another—as Hulk Hogan and Randy Savage did in the events that formed their tag team partnership—to find that a friend in need is a friend in deed. At *WrestleMania IV* (1988), Hulk Hogan aided and applauded Randy Savage's victory, embracing him and miming putting the championship belt around his own waist as Miss Elizabeth watched tearfully. For the next episode, *SummerSlam* (1988), the two men appeared in matching yellow (Hulk Hogan's signature color) briefs with

"*★MEGA★ POWERS*" printed across the buttocks. Attending them was Miss Elizabeth in a dress of equivalent color. The victory was won when Savage forced (heel) guest referee Jesse "the Body" Ventura to count out the Million Dollar Man, and the celebration included a lengthy embrace between Hogan and Miss Elizabeth. The relationship between the two men was further developed through a series of similar episodes in which their bond was made visible and idealized in their mutual support and succor in action, in their matching trunks and shared gestures of appreciation, in their manly handshakes and manly embrace. From the start the bond and its progressive disintegration was both reflected in and legitimized by the admiring tears of Miss Elizabeth.

In his discussion of wrestling's melodramatic structure, Henry Jenkins points to the representation of interdependence in the tag team match: "WWF wrestling operates along the gap that separates our cultural ideal of male autonomy and the reality of alienation. . . . The fighter, that omnipotent muscle machine, steps alone, with complete confidence, into the ring, ready to do battle with his opponent. As the fight progresses, he is beaten down, unable to manage without assistance. Struggling to the ropes, he must admit that he needs another man. His partner reaches out to him, while he crawls along the floor, inching towards that embrace" (31). This display of need and reciprocity, as Jenkins points out, can readily be read as a display of desire between men, the point at which violence and intimacy become inextricably linked (32). At the same time, the perils of intimacy between men inevitably emerge in tag team performance. The uniting of two men in partnership is as necessary as its dissolution in the wrestling event. What the wrestler discovers and reaches for is another man like him, his apparent double in virtue (or vice), one with whom he bonds (at least temporarily) in a partnership that is not unlike a marriage with equivalent problematics. As the desire for the connection with the other man surfaces, the ambivalence toward intimacy between men emerges and converges with homophobia.

Tag-teaming starts with expressions of homosociability and comes to skirt both homoeroticism and homophobia. Partners embrace each other—the Bushwackers go so far as to lick each other's faces—and avow their undying love for and support for one another. If one partner is injured, the other rushes to defend, succor, and avenge. But, as with Hogan and Savage, their fallings-out are portrayed as the result of the inevitable tensions that occur when two powerful men become "intimate" as partners rather than as opponents. The betrayal of one partner by another creates a hostility that extends expressively beyond the professional into the realm of the rejected lover, and the resulting grudge, like a masculine soap opera, provides the material for a new story line.

In the wrestling performance, sexuality is always commingled with violence. The central visual image is the apparently conflictual but actually mutual embrace of two men. Indeed, what we see repeatedly as the struggle reaches its resolution is one man mounting, or attempting to mount, the prone body of the other. The sexual synergy lurking within the play of dominance and submission may indeed be, as Larry Brisco once told me, like "making love to a woman" (interview 1993) in that the wrestler seeks to seduce and manipulate the responses of the (feminized) spectator, but as the action itself is between men it is also manifestly homoerotic—or, again using DeGaris's term, "homosensual." The exchange both overtly and covertly conflates violence with lovemaking. Its effect is a revel celebrated by nearly naked men in skintight Lycra who hold, release, and throw their opponents to the mat, finally "covering" them in the victory gesture that also climaxes the act. The most violent postures are also the most apparently sexual, as when one man takes the other's head between his legs, turning him upside down in a "pile driver" that often leaves the victim unconscious and ready for the final pin.

This visual display of physical intimacy between men is reinforced by the verbal taunting that justifies and contextualizes each match. Wrestlers frequently articulate their challenges in terms that verge on the sexual as they describe in detail what they will do once they get their hands on each other. Consequently, Hulk Hogan's vehement denial of inappropriate desire for Miss Elizabeth included an insistence that Savage keep the quarrel between men that seems explicitly (homo)sexual: "Yes, I've got lust," Hogan growled, "but it's not for Elizabeth. I've got lust for *you,* Macho Man" (*WWF Superstars of Wrestling* 22 April 1989). To Savage's new partner, Zeus, Hogan also issued a challenge that was charged with (homo)sexual implications: "I want to know if you can handle the largest arms in the world around your waist" (*WWF Wrestling Challenge* 27 August 1989). In the macho rhetoric of wrestling, such words—especially as they point to the breakdown in a formerly intimate partnership—clearly muscle the opponent into the feminine position, threaten emasculation through sexual domination, and consequently bring to the surface the undercurrents in wrestling that are simultaneously homosocial, homoerotic, and homophobic.

Like Gorgeous George and Ricky Starr, some wrestlers flirt with or overtly display wrestling's (homo)sexual vocabularies more visibly and/or aggressively than others. The performance of Ravishing Rick Rude in the late 1980s and early 1990s provides a paradigm of wrestling's conflation of the feminine and masculine markers, working within a camp aesthetic that is somehow at once hetero- and homosexual, within a tradition that critic Sam Fussell recognizes as the bodybuilder tradition: "simultaneously bully and sissy, butch and femme" (44). Rude always entered to "the Stripper," flaunting glitzy robes and aggressively demanding that his audience submit its admiration to "the sexiest man alive" before stripping and flexing in full bodybuilder drag. He also often wore his opponent's likeness on his crotch or buttocks, and his struts were punctuated by hip thrusts to the audience or a gluteus flex that obscenely manipulated his opponent's cartooned features. His signature finish—the "rude awakening"—explicitly conflated a sexual insult to his vanquished opponent with a display of mastery over a woman.

Yet Rude's display of the hyperdeveloped male body within the flamboyance of sequins and gestures and his claim to sexual as well as gladiatorial prowess sustained apparently irreconcilable contradictions. His performance was at once excessive and disciplined, presenting the results of years of hard work on his body as an artifact that was both powerful and genuinely obscene, in a performance verging on the pornographic. In displaying his hypermasculine body as an object to be admired and desired he also declared himself as a man to be anything but passive, a "cock of the walk" capable of conquering men and women alike. His aggressive conflation of masculine and feminine, of gay and straight aesthetics was extraordinarily successful in generating what can only be recognized as genuine heel heat: spectators hated him. Indeed, one man at a WWF match in Madison Square Garden told my husband very seriously that he no longer brings his kids to matches because of Rude's moves, adding a homophobic comment that made it clear that his antagonism was a direct response to Rude's blatant exploitation of wrestling's otherwise covert homosexual imagery.

Still, a wrestler who appropriates and explicitly displays the markers of homosexual camp is not automatically denied face status. Indeed, as DeGaris points out, the historical and contemporary relationship of performers and audiences to homoeroticism and homosexuality is far less straightforward and far more fluid than is generally assumed ("Professional Wrestling's Commercial Exploitation of Homophobia"). In practice, then and now, it is not enough to say that the manly man will be favored over the feminine. In the 1950s and 1960s Gorgeous George, with his performance of the clichés of homosexuality, may indeed have been an incitement to expressions of homophobia. Certainly, his superstardom was intimately connected to the audience's pleasure in jeering his feminine posturing. But if Ricky Starr, whose ballet-dancer performance presents an equivalent assault on the idea of the manly man, was hugely popular at the same time, cheered as he literally danced circles around his macho opponents, then surely the audience's sense of complicity in his mockery must have been evoked along with, and even superseded, its potential antipathy toward his portrayal of the unmasculine man.

In his exploration of wrestling's more ambiguous relationship to homosexuality, DeGaris discusses a recent WWF star Goldust (Dustin Runnels) who openly displays the homophobe's canon of homosexual clichés as part of his efforts to generate and sustain heel heat. According to DeGaris, Goldust regularly "makes sexual advances to a usually well muscled good guy wrestler. The good guy becomes enraged and disgusted at Goldust's advances and retaliates by pro wrestling's equivalent of 'fag bashing' " (6). The controversy has even surfaced in the *New York Times Magazine* (22 September 1996), which presents the protests of several gay rights groups next to the picture of a sneering transvestite in platinum wig and boa, with white face and darkly painted eyes and lips. Yet in contrast to the *Times'* anticipation that given Goldust's status as "the Most Hated Wrestler in the biz" the character will "die a natural death," DeGaris speculates that the next step for Goldust will be a face turn. After describing a number of provocative story lines in which Goldust has crossed the line from homosexual insinuation into action—touching and propositioning the Ultimate Warrior, attempting to administer "mouth to mouth" to an unconscious Ahmed Johnson, and so on—DeGaris points to the increasing size of Goldust's small but visible and vocal cheering section. He thus acknowledges the way in which the wrestling's developmental patterns will tend to supersede the details of characterization and speculates that "it will be interesting to see if Goldust will be able to change the meaning of his homoerotic persona and gain fan approval" (9). Given that Goldust has been increasingly positioned as a protector of various women, it appears more than likely that this face turn will be attached to a representation of Goldust's emergent heterosexual side. Consequently, the turn will carry with it conservative if not homophobic implications as his essential masculinity is revealed as essential heterosexuality. But it is also clear that the promotion would not give him a push toward hero status if his popularity were not already perceptible. Indeed, as I write this a heated debate currently ongoing in the RSPW discussion is focused not on if but when and how Goldust will turn face within the coming year.

The wrestling aesthetic closely commingles a display of violence with obvious sexual imagery that goes well beyond flaunting the male physique and physical capabilities for female admiration. Indeed, the masculinity presented in wrestling is not limited to or inhibited by the expectations of female spectators and players. Women as they appear in the wrestling discourse may necessarily be nominally and figuratively the target of much of the wrestlers' sexual strutting and posturing. But it is "real" women who are effectively excluded from wrestling's economic and erotic exchanges except insofar as they serve to reinforce the wrestlers' masculine identities. In particular as "real" women enter into the display as objects of desire, they authenticate the wrestlers' heterosexuality and as such provide nonhomosexual ways of bridging the distance between men. It is "real" women who, like Miss Elizabeth and the showgirls at Caesar's Palace, hold the mirror up to the wrestler's masculine image. And it is "real" women—wrestlers, managers and valets, and fans alike—who inevitably occupy the place of the "not-so-real" man, the antithesis to masculine identity, as even a Gorgeous George or a Goldust comes to reveal and revel in his claim to masculine prowess.

As the performers of professional wrestling mask their profound dependence upon and cooperation with each other in the ring with their hypermasculine displays of violence, so too they perform a denial of intimacy even as their performances are exceptionally, provocatively intimate. The irreconcilable tension in the ring is between the idea(l) of the man who stands alone and that of the man who stands with other men. A "real" man relies on his own strength and skill, but he also must at times rely on others. The pleasures of partnership with another man and the joy of seeing himself reflected in another like him is always superseded by the drive to the top of the ladder and the fear that the other man will prove to be more man than he is. What is at stake in each match is nothing less than a man's identity as a man, his masculinity, and it is the underlying threat of emasculation that provides much of wrestling's ongoing heat. No matter how evenly matched the men appear to be—as in the matchups between Luger and Perfect, and Michaels and Ramon— the test of manhood inevitably results in a loss for one of them. It is, then, the idea of the "feminine"—the submission side of the play of dominance and submission—that is resisted for real in the ring. It is one thing for Gorgeous George to flaunt his curls, Ricky Starr his ballet slippers, Lex Luger his muscles, and Shawn Michaels his charms. But in the exchange of position between the "not-so-real" man and the "real" man—even if, and especially when, the "not-so-real" man loses the match—it is imperative for each wrestler that his drag is dropped at some point to display and celebrate the essential man within.

Chapter Five

FROM BEEFCAKE TO CHEESECAKE

Missy will put herself in a man's place and be treated like a
man.

—Paul E. Dangerously

Now we'll get down to *wrestling*. Get her out of the building.
She never belonged in the first place.

—Jesse "the Body" Ventura

"If the guy starts to get sexual—if I hear him doing things, or if he
puts a woman on the telephone—I hang up. I don't do phone sex.
I'm a feminist." Sky Magic is explaining "phone wrestling"—a
man calls a 900 number, she verbally wrestles with him, he pays by the
minute—as we ride together from Brooklyn to Manhattan on the F Train
(2 August 1993). The only woman I saw working out with the wrestlers
at Gleason's regularly during my visits, Sky is in superb physical condition; her compact, tightly muscled and disciplined body is the outward
manifestation of several years of competitive bodybuilding as well as
side-training in karate and kick-boxing. When I returned to Gleason's in
1993 after an extended absence, she had been training with Johnny for
about a month. At our first meeting, she welcomed me warmly as "another woman" and, in much the same vein as the men, on occasion urged
me to attempt a bit of training myself. Sky and I were not necessarily

any more inclined toward intimacy or bonding as one woman with another than we were as women with the men, although she would consistently make a point of sitting with me for a bit of conversation whenever there was an opportunity. I was then, and remain in retrospect, impressed by her discipline and her acumen, by her willingness and ability to enter into training on the wrestlers' terms.

At the time I knew her (1993–94), Sky was actually managing to earn an income from her identity as a bodybuilder and wrestler, primarily through enterprises not available to the male wrestlers. As she told me on the subway, she regularly "wrestles" men who call a 900 number for which she is paid ten dollars per hour. With occasional work in "apartment house wrestling," she tells me, it's enough to get by. Apartment house wrestling is evidently quite lucrative, paying a woman up to three hundred dollars an hour for going to a man's apartment and wrestling with him for a set period of time. She is emphatic: she refuses to do anything sexual. She's not prostituting herself. She's a feminist. Her ongoing objective, and the reason she started training as a wrestler, is to earn money as an athlete, to be paid for developing and working with her body as she desires. On these terms, it is logical, albeit somewhat ironic, that Sky Magic might be considered one of the few truly "professional" wrestlers at Gleason's.

Apartment house wrestling? Telephone wrestling? I am absolutely flabbergasted. I ask my questions in a flurry of astonishment: You keep your clothes on? You just wrestle with the guy in his living room? He keeps his clothes on? You just describe the moves on the phone, like "Now I've got you in a headlock" or "Now I've pinned you to the mat, and the referee is counting you out?" She responds "Yes" to all my questions, at the same time reiterating that she is a feminist. After a bit of ad hoc research—scouring the phone sex advertisements in the back of the *Village Voice,* leafing through old wrestling magazines, e-mailing a friend who has been a phone sex worker off and on for many years—I come to believe her. Given that actual phone sex workers generally earn seven to twelve dollars per twenty minutes, it is in fact possible that Sky, who earns far less, is telling the truth about her prohibition against sexual talk. But the line between phone wrestling and phone sex is rather ambiguous. Beyond the advertisements for bondage and domination calls, I am told by my friend that the businesses she works for often offer their clients a "two-girl call, which wrestling calls are most of the time" and which pays the same seven to twelve dollars each "and costs the guy anywhere from $60 on, depending on add-ons. S&M is an add-on, for example, or incest" (Sonntag, e-mail correspondence 9 December 1996). In fact, as I learn much later, women wrestlers often do cross over from athletic into erotic display in a variety of ways—from selling photographs of the cheesecake or nude variety to performing in explicitly pornographic videos.

The performance of female wrestlers—even or perhaps especially when it is most like the performance of male wrestlers—invariably gen-

"ROCK HARD STRONG AND SEXY" (Advertisement from *Village Voice*, 5 July 1994)

"Grab the Scoop!" (Advertisement from *Wrestling World,* March 1990) erates its heat as much from its implied (if not actualized) erotics as from its athletics and from its legitimizing effect on men's wrestling. From my own position as a woman at ringside, the implications of Sky's revelations about her income-producing occupations appear at once obvious and contradictory, truthful and suspect on many levels. Consequently, it is important to acknowledge that in her assertion that she is a feminist who maintains her personal and professional integrity while selling her services over the telephone and in men's apartments Sky Magic is telling the truth. At least, she is telling the truth insofar as she is claiming a kind of propriety, both in establishing the limits of her accommodation to the client's desire and in claiming ownership of her body and identity in performance. At the same time, regardless of the way in which she represents her actions, when I consider her acts of display and commodification I remain ambivalent. If it is true in theatrical performance, as Laurence Senelick has observed, that "to appear on stage is to display one's body to strangers: A commodity available to the gaze may, in given circumstances, be vendible in its entirety" (xii), then surely it is even more true that the display of the female body in a male-dominated sports performance would be commodified (that is, sexualized) regardless of what is performed.

If anything, given the ways in which the discourses of the squared circle and its performers are explicitly gendered—male and female, masculine and feminine, hetero- and homosexual—professional wrestling, even more than other forms of performance, must be inflected by what Senelick identifies as the stage's "prostitutional aspect" (xii). By marketing herself as a phone and apartment house wrestler as well as a performer, Sky has effectively translated the masculinist discourse of professional wrestling—its display of the male body in violent physical contact—into an economically viable feminine (if not feminist) discourse. Paradoxically, as a woman working in the squared circle she has become a "professional" in ways that are simultaneously like and unlike the men. She stands uneasily between identification with the professional man—someone who earns a living at a chosen occupation, one requiring a degree of training, skill, and experience—and that implied by the more colloquial usage of the word when applied to women—someone stereotypically identified as a "working girl" or prostitute.

That is to say, what Sky performs is not necessarily what is seen. What she sells is her bodybuilder's physique and wrestler's physicality according to the protocols of her profession. What promoters, spectators, and clients buy is not necessarily the same thing. What she sells, what men pay for, apparently, is an idea of her body in action, which is erotically stimulating for its having to do with conventions of the strong and/or dominant woman, with ideas of bondage and discipline, of sadomasochism at a very simple, simplistic level. What she sells, what men buy, apparently, is a kind of safe sex twice removed, in which sexual intimacy is, apparently, limited to intimation and imagination rather than performed as such. As a working "girl wrestler," Sky may not be prostituting herself in the street sense—I do believe her when she insists that she does not have sex with her clients—but what she sells and what men buy is nonetheless sex, or perhaps more precisely a particular idea of sex.

Clearly, the performance of the female wrestler—"girl wrestler" is actually the more common term—is multilayered and ambivalently marked. The distinction I am drawing between what women wrestlers do as perceived both by women and by men in wrestling and what spectators pay for is neither obvious nor easy. Indeed, Larry DeGaris is critical of my reading of difference, "In Gleason's, women have not upset the applecart. In fact, *serious* women . . . are seen as helping to legitimate what the men do" (DeGaris, e-mail correspondence 27 January 1997, emphasis his). But in fact it is the way in which the appearance of women in wrestling—as wrestlers, as manager/consorts, and as spectators— serves to legitimate wrestling's masculine discourse that has become most problematic and consequently most intriguing for me as a woman watching from ringside.

The presence of the woman wrestler is bound up in conventionally eroticized ideas of female power, the sale of her performance conflated simultaneously with male desire to see two women "together" and with male desire to experience domination without danger. If the performances of male wrestlers may be seen to celebrate a range of masculine possibilities while affirming the essential "man" within, then it is possible to see that the performances of female wrestlers also serve to celebrate and affirm masculine ideals. The performance of the girl wrestler serves to legitimate the male wrestler's performance both by taking the place of the "not-man" and by deflecting the event's otherwise homoerotic energies onto herself. At the same time, in doing exactly what the men do in performance, she also serves to bring to the surface the otherwise repressed sexual implications of the wrestling event.

Moreover, whereas the pleasure peculiar to the wrestling event for men as participants and spectators may be grounded in the wide range of masculine identifications available for admiration and imitation, for women the terrain may be limited, less a matter of license than of limitation. While the characters developed by male wrestlers are clearly identifiable in cultural stereotypes—the businessman, the millionaire, the high school jock, the surfer, the biker, and so forth—the characterization of women in wrestling remains for the most part abstract. Instead of being particular to specific types of women in everyday life, their roles are circumscribed by dominant cultural clichés of the virgin/whore binary. They are either "good girls" or "bad girls," chaste and self-denying or promiscuous and self-serving, Miss Elizabeth or Scary Sherri. Even in these terms, whether in the big leagues or in local shows, women appear only sporadically as wrestlers, usually only one match at most will feature women in a given event. Instead women most often appear as consorts, as managers or valets, to the male wrestlers. Thus, although female performers (wrestlers and managers) participate along the same lines as male performers in the play of virtue and vice as faces or heels, their performances are always reflective of sexual status and defined in relation to the men with whom they are associated.

Like Sky, the male wrestlers, promoters, and many hard-core fans male and female alike insist that there is no difference between the way in which men train and perform and the way in which women train and perform. In the words of one female fan: "Do you really see Francine the Manager as a 'helpless' female? IMO [in my opinion], and I'm thinking in the context of the storyline, Francine is getting *into the ring* with the wrestlers. In my mind that is where the line is crossed. . . . I agree that it isn't pleasant to see her getting knocked around, but when someone gets into that ring, they had better be prepared to accept what happens. If you're helpless, if you can't be a warrior, stay out" (Carrington 13 December 1996). The rules of the game, its moves and values, they insist, are exactly the same. A woman engages with the men in displaying violence on the same terms, with neither accommodation nor acknowledgment of difference. A warrior is a warrior, regardless of gender.

The distinction between men and women in wrestling is not in the wrestling per se, but in the ways in which the spectacle of women wrestling is staged and framed for an audience and situated in the dominant culture. In the wrestling itself the unspoken rules—about touching without actually touching, about being touched without being touched—that the male wrestler assimilates in his early weeks, are easily extended from man-to-man workouts to physical contact between men and women. What, after all, is the difference in the kind of sexual denial required of a man in training or performance in order, for example, to reach through another man's legs or a woman's legs as part of what one wrestling manual calls "center-step penetration" (Jarman and Hanley 102), between the denial of the possibility of homosexual desire and the denial of the possibility of heterosexual desire in such intimate encounters?

Indeed, Sky's training was, as the wrestlers insisted, virtually identical to that of the men. She would arrive, warm up with stretches, falls, push-ups, and an astonishing series of chin-ups, and then stand at ringside waiting for a chance to work out. The men would acknowledge her arrival as any other, then return to what they were doing, inviting her in as the workout progressed. On one such typical day, Rubio and Frankie had had an extended period in the ring to themselves. Earlier I had watched Rubio teach Frankie an apparently complex series of acrobatic moves. When Sky arrived, they gave her a lesson that was remarkable primarily because she learned what had in the beginning appeared impossibly complex—a leap to the shoulders, followed by a curve down and pull through the opponent's legs, a twist and a pin—in an exceptionally short period of time, perhaps an hour. Her speedy learning curve is attributable to her superb physical condition, to her disciplined approach to learning moves, to whatever kinetic fluencies had accrued to her from previous training, as well as to the men's seriousness in instructing, guiding, and correcting her. While the men were obviously pleased to be exchanging moves with someone new, and everyone was exhausted at the end, it certainly seemed from outside the ring that the focus had never shifted from the physical to the sexual. The work was the work. There were no sexual innuendoes played out physically or verbally, not even the occasional oblique veiled reference to the potentially provocative contact at hand.

Yet there is a distinct difference between men wrestling and "girl wrestlers." If this difference is not to be located in the actual physical practices of the wrestlers, in the way they touch, understand, and express the significance of touching each other, then it must be found in the way in which the act of wrestling is perceived from outside the ring, by promoters and spectators. The role of women in the ring, like that of men, is

Sky Magic gets a lesson in Lucha Libre from Rubio and Frankie (pages 125 and 126).

no less reflective of cultural assumptions about masculine and feminine propriety, about how real and not-so-real, good and not-so good, women are to be recognized. That is, the role of women in wrestling, as in other performance practices, is framed by the culture itself, in the act of looking as it is generally practiced, in the idea of wrestling as a masculine performance art, and in the arena as a site of meaning constructed by and for men. Although the women may train with and in ways identical to the men, with the same diffusion/denial of erotic tension and anxiety, their value in professional wrestling's erotic economy is always sexualized in a way that is markedly different from that of the male wrestlers. No matter how directly a woman's moves may replicate those of the men in the ring—and as in Sky's case even at some distance from the ring, over the telephone or in a man's living room—the performance of the "girl wrestler" must be seen as both parodic and pornographic, an imitation of what men do that is, by definition, sexually provocative.

Soon after beginning my research at Gleason's in 1989 I attended one of Johnny's regular public exhibitions. I was sitting in the audience diligently taking notes and photographs when a girl wrestler—the first I had seen there—named Linda Dallas grabbed the microphone from the announcer and shouted "Brooklyn sucks!" While this gesture might have been made by any of the male wrestlers and would have rightly been judged as cheap heat, with little more required to position her as a heel against a Brooklyn audience, the nature of the crowd's invective shifted radically as she began to wrestle. Yes, they were jeering her as she shook her fists and yelled her insults. And yes, they cheered her opponent, Misty Blue, when she turned to them for approbation and encouragement. But whereas throughout the earlier matches the voices were balanced between those of male and female spectators, now the bulk of the responses were from the men. The women appeared to have disappeared; they had gone to the ladies room, were getting more beer for themselves and their husbands, or were talking to their children and amongst themselves. For their part, while the men carried on the call and response, they were no longer shouting the customary directives to kill or maim, but were instead yelling obscene sexual challenges at both women.

It was no longer a family show. Both women were treated to graphic descriptions of which sexual acts the men in the audience thought they were worth. Any consideration of the differences between the two performers seemed to be displaced from evaluations of their not-inconsiderable athletic prowess. What was most apparent was the high degree of sexual hostility and aggression directed toward both of them. Linda Dallas as the heel may have generated the greatest negative heat, but Misty Blue was no less targeted with a wide array of sexual come-ons. Even the referee participated in the sexual gaming, at one point carefully pulling one woman's leotard from where it had bunched into her buttocks and stretching it to cover her more modestly, all the while rolling his eyes and wincing directly at and in complicity with the audience. Further, while the souvenir photos for sale at the side table featured the men in mock or serious fighting poses, Misty Blue's photo with its ripped t-shirt and sexual come-on was pure cheesecake. Indeed, as I discover later, the fan trade in lewd and nude photos of female wrestlers and managers is astonishingly prolific. While there is a brisk fan trade in costumed posed and action photographs of male wrestlers and managers, no parallel pornographic phenomenon exists. Whereas in the past, the women more or less controlled and profited from the display of their bodies, their images are now bandied about the Internet for anyone to download, and requests for nude photos of whomever is hot are common, often daily occurrences in the rec.sport.pro-wrestling newsgroup.

In the match between Linda Dallas and Misty Blue, the performance of each hold ultimately seemed designed more to expose the women's bodies to the audience in a series of sexually provocative freeze-frames—breasts pulled tight against Lycra, buttocks suspended through the ropes, and so on—than as part of a progression toward victory. What was being performed were literally the moves and holds of professional wrestling. But as the performance mimicked what men do in the squared circle, ironically it became possible to see it also as nothing so much as a mimicking of the kinds of pornography that feature representations of lesbians coupling for a presumptive male audience. That is, the match between Linda Dallas and Misty Blue in the end parodied both wrestling and pornography, and it was received as such by the audience.[1]

Whatever a woman's formal role in the wrestling event might be, as spectator, manager, or wrestler, her function is always to affirm male heterosexual orthodoxy. As spectators, women become the nominal targets of the male wrestler's sexual energy, his struts and his come-ons, a site for the displacement of the homoerotic dynamic. As managers, women bridge and shape the gap between spectators and wrestlers, at

Linda Dallas chokes Misty Blue in ropes.

once acting as spectators to and markers for the relative masculinity of the wrestlers. Although as wrestlers, women may temporarily occupy the central position of the male-defined space, their performances ultimately intersect the pornographic with the male audience's response predictably, and aggressively, obscene. In the end, while women in wrestling are free to act *as* men, what they are, ultimately, is *not* men.

In order to understand the way in which women are typically positioned in the wrestling event it may be useful to return to the example of Ravishing Rick Rude, whose WWF performances in the late 1980s and early 1990s as a heel were defined by, and the heat he generated was in large part owing to, his blatant toying with the otherwise suppressed (homo)sexual tensions of the ring. He was, if it is possible to conceive of such a thing, a more aggressive, more degenerate version of Gorgeous George. Upon entering the ring, he would appropriate the announcer's microphone to issue a challenge that generally ran something like "I want all you soft dough-boys in the audience to take a look at the body that is driving your wives and girlfriends wild with desire" before stripping off his sequined robe and flexing his abdominal muscles to the tune

Misty Blue: publicity photo.

of "The Stripper." From beginning to end of Rude's performances, male spectators would hoot and scream and carry on, affirming their hatred of Rude with astonishing ferocity. In contrast, the television cameras would show the female spectators exuberantly laughing along with, as well as jeering at, his posing provocations throughout. Crucial to Rude's performance was his signature hold, the "rude awakening" (a basic sleeper hold), which culminated with the vanquished opponent prone on the mat while he gyrated his hips rudely over the man's face and upper torso. Following this version of the "rude awakening" would be another in which a young woman would be brought into the ring for an extended kiss. She would then swoon, finishing prone and apparently unconscious on the mat while Rude again gyrated his hips over her face and upper torso. One display of prowess was succeeded by another, the subduing of one opponent through apparent physical violence followed by the subduing of another through apparent sexual mastery, if not violation.

The temporary introjection of a female spectator into the playing area was not at all superfluous to Rick Rude's performance. Obviously, the woman's entrance as the desiring one, along with her swoon at his kiss, served as final proof of his claims of athletic and sexual prowess. More important, however, the appearance of the female spectator served simultaneously to make visible and to displace the homoerotic anxieties implicit in Rude's performance. That is, the double-gendered "rude awakening" conflated the two forms of physical contact, the violent and the sexual; it made the male opponent equivalent to the female and the dominance of one, like the other, both violently aggressive and intensely sexualized. At the same time, Rude's vulgar sexual insult to his vanquished opponent might be seen to extend to the female spectator and then, ironically, to ricochet back to the male opponent once more. That is, the male opponent ultimately appeared equivalent to the female spectator, his unconscious capitulation reflected in the feminine swoon in response and contrast to the display of virile masculinity by the victor. In Rude's sexual coda, expressive violence between men became interchangeable with expressive desire between men and women, the performance of one type of embrace not much different from the other.

Given the masculinist ideology of the ring, it is perhaps not surprising that Rude's rudely exposed sexual expressivity attracted an equivalently virulent response from male spectators. Nor was the mocking laughter of the women out of line with the conventions of the ring. Although women

Ring girl with placard at *Monday Night RAW*.

Longtime fan with placard at *Monday Night RAW*.

certainly participate in the event on similar terms to the men, particularly in acquiring and displaying knowledge of the game and the players, the relationship of the female spectators to the performance can diverge in ways that are both more overtly sexual and more playful. The wrestling audience is almost equally divided between men and women. Female fans are as widely varied as male fans, from young women and teenagers to elderly ladies, from those who appear to attend in order to ogle and express desire for the men to those who appear to want to be like the men, and from the mostly anonymous fans to the most well-known to wrestlers and spectators: women like Hatpin Mary, who (as her name implies) in the days when women wore hats, was known to stick male wrestlers when they fell out of the ring, or more recently, the pair of sisters who according to gossip have spent so much time avidly following the WWF and hanging out after matches that they have been given lifetime passes and who have even appeared in the ring alternating with other more conventionally provocative ring girls wearing swimsuits and carrying placards at *Monday Night RAW*.[2]

While the relationship of male spectators to the wrestling event appears to retain at least a vestige of the idea of a sporting event—with a serious kind of keeping score and evaluation of performance on athletic terms paralleling their participation in the play—female spectators tend toward a more carnivalesque relationship to the performance. In fact, it is possible to say that the difference in wrestling between male and female spectators is much like the difference between male and female watchers of striptease. Chad Dell, in his exploration of the relationship of female fans to professional wrestling during the postwar era (1945–60), also makes this comparison: "Yet long before male strip shows became commonplace, genres such as professional wrestling provided the context for women to publicly exhibit sexual desire, whether real or feigned—or at least freedom from the disavowal of desire—and transgress the norms of 'acceptable' female sexual behavior." Moreover, as Dell further speculates, it is possible that "much of the pleasure involved had more to do with the act of participation itself than with supposed 'object' of their affections" (18).

As spectators, women are the nominal targets for the male wrestlers' sexual energies, while as participants, they become the explicit targets for the male spectators' sexual energies. In both positions, the dynamic is exceptionally ambivalent, a throwback to clichés of the war between the sexes in which women are understood by men to be a necessary evil: simultaneously objects of desire and intruders, always potentially disruptive and destructive of male order. If the performance of professional wrestling is a "man's game" and in this regard acts as a macrocosmic representation of the masculine world, then the presence of women as both spectators and participants is simultaneously essential to, and a problematic in, the erotic economy of the ring. The presence of women on both sides of the squared circle provides a focal point for the affirmation of heterosexual dominance by male participants. At the same time, women are always intruders into an explicitly masculinist culture where the feminine position for men and women alike is one of degradation and corruption. Women as watchers represent the appropriately heterosexual other in the male wrestlers' displays, allowing the wrestler to assert that he is not exposing his body for the approbation of other men per se by directing his sexual orientation past the other men toward the female. Women as direct participants always come to represent a threat to masculine virtue, either as an incitement to desire and thus distraction from the work of wrestling or by contaminating the wrestler who attaches himself to her with her less than manly values. The feminine woman is to be idealized and the more masculine woman resisted, but both are ultimately represented as outsiders, who must be pushed away from the masculine epicenter with force. In the end, even Miss Elizabeth is a destabilizing, destructive presence in the ring, and her dismissal is ultimately required to clear the way for the victory of virtue at *Wrestle-Mania V*.

Like the male wrestlers, the women who perform as wrestlers and/or managers explicitly represent themselves as virtuous or sinister. In many ways the terms by which a woman can be identified as a face or heel can be seen as consistent with those for men. To be a face a woman must present herself as someone who both plays by the rules and is respectful of authority. Like men who wrestle or manage as faces, the woman must explicitly align herself with, and fight for, the spectators. And like men, to be a heel as a wrestler or manager, a woman simply presents herself in opposition to, and performs against, these ideals. But as in life, in professional wrestling the terms by which virtuous women are distinguished from the nonvirtuous are always at least implicitly sexual. At the same time that she operates within the hero/villain binary, a woman in the arena must balance the conventional codes of feminine virtue against the masculine codes of honor. A woman must, that is, perform her role in a way that parallels or opposes the masculine ideal while conforming to the dominant culture's idea of femininity.

What shifts then is the nature of the dialectic itself: while men conform to performance codes in relation to other men and are defined as masculine in a masculine-defined world, women must perform as women in relation to men and are defined as feminine in a masculine-defined world. A woman's entrance, by definition, explicitly sexualizes the performance according to standards of heterosexual orthodoxy. Her performance must either be recognizable as "feminine" (that is, soft-spoken and accommodating to the men to whom she is attached, acting often as another outward sign of the man's virtue) or "not-feminine" (that is, loud and confrontational, and if attached to a man appearing as the visible manifestation of his moral corruption).

Given the degree to which the spectacle of dominance and submission between men is underscored with erotic sensibilities, it is not surprising then that a woman's appearance would threaten to destabilize the event by bringing these sensibilities to the surface. The performance of normative feminine ideals in the context of the ring is obviously and fundamentally incompatible with wrestling's hypermasculine codes of honor. Insofar as the performance of normative feminine ideals is conflated with and perceived as the performance of feminine sexuality in relation to masculine integrity, the presence of women in the ring always carries with it the potential to disrupt and destabilize. Indeed, it is possible to assert that when a woman occupies the ring or ringside for any length of time, her ability to embody femininity as an ideal inevitably decays. Once this conversion to the representation of the dangerous woman occurs, unlike with male wrestlers, a reconversion to the place of virtue is unlikely. Like the restoration of virginity itself, a return to innocence for a woman in wrestling is virtually impossible. She becomes a virago, or worse, and the men who come into contact with her risk potential contamination and/or unjust losses.

In a televised broadcast of Ted Turner's World Championship Wrestling, which I caught only obliquely several years ago, the story of a new female manager and the subsequent degradation of the male wrestler was recapped as follows: The wrestler, a face, was down in the ring when a woman emerged from the audience to distract his opponent and thus save him from sure defeat. They quickly became an item—that is, it was implied, developed a sexual relationship—and as a result the wrestler became less inclined to follow the rules and explicitly shunned the audience instead of asking for their support. Clearly the woman, from her first intervention, was to blame for the decline and corruption of the wrestler. As was demonstrated in the WCW broadcast, while close proximity to the woman was the downfall of the man, the woman herself was infected by her close proximity to the heady masculine world of professional wrestling. From her first appearance as a courageous and still sweet onlooker, one who identified with and took action in support of the virtuous man, she was transformed, becoming "THE WOMAN" (all in caps as the subtitles proclaimed): a vamp in slinky dresses who aggressively interfered in subsequent matches. In the broadcast, the announcer played a tape of a recent interview in which THE WOMAN is seen to have kept him waiting, demanding more champagne, approaching him with unveiled sexual innuendoes, and generally harassing him until he made his escape.

In the WWF the appearance of women as performer/players was generally confined to two in the late 1980s and early 1990s: the "lovely" Miss Elizabeth, a manager, and "Sensational" (or "Scary") Sherri, a wrestler as well as manager. Matches featuring women wrestlers are sporadically presented at best, usually with Alundra Blaze, who has appeared on occasion as the female titleholder, although without much of a story line or angle as context. Known as the "first lady of wrestling" Miss Elizabeth usually appears as a manager on the side of the good guy: first for Macho Man Randy Savage (to whom she was married for a time) and then, when Savage turned heel, for Hulk Hogan. In contrast, Sherri is almost exclusively attached to heels—for example, appearing as consort to Savage in his bad-guy phase.

Miss Elizabeth always dresses in what might be described as upscale valley girl party dresses and is presented as both nurturing and needing protection. Her sexuality is directly linked to the man she manages, but always chastely within the bounds of propriety. Sherri vamps in black or white parodies of the tramp-vampire genre, with sequins festooning both her costume and her elaborately and brightly painted face. She is fickle in her affection, selling her services to the highest bidder, takes a very active role in helping her wrestler cheat his way to victory—for a time the gimmick of choice was an apparently brick-laden evening bag—and is often pointed to as the cause of the downfall of a virtuous man. With her provocative performances, she often becomes the target of vehement fan antipathy. According to one recent account by a woman who might be considered a longtime, hard-core wrestling fan: "I went to a WWF show at the Cow Palace back in '90, and Scary Sherri Martel was managing . . . someone (the memory is the first thing to go!). I've never seen *anyone* get pelted with stuff the way she did! Full cups of beer, cokes, buckets of popcorn, trash . . . you name it. And it was not staged—fans were doing the throwing. The security staff did their best to catch all the throwers, and when they did, they were escorted out, none too gently" (Carrington 12 December 1996).

In 1991 the two women took center stage for an extended scenario that culminated in the "wedding" of Miss Elizabeth and Randy Savage during *SummerSlam* at Madison Square Garden, a story line that generated tremendous heat in the buildup to the event, even though the two had actually been married since the early 1980s.[3] Savage's proposal to Miss Elizabeth was repeatedly featured and elaborated upon in a series of televised broadcasts over many months. According to the story line, Savage and Miss Elizabeth had been estranged for a long period of time, and Sherri had supplanted Elizabeth as manager/consort, when he went up against the Ultimate Warrior in the *WrestleMania VII* "retirement match" in which the stakes dictated that the loser would be forced to retire from wrestling. When Savage lost, Sherri leapt to the ring and expressed her contempt by pummeling him, pulling his hair and kicking him, in the words of one commentator, "further humiliating this great grappler in his lowest moment" (Krebs 29). Miss Elizabeth, who conveniently happened to be watching in the audience, "rushed to ringside, jumped over the guardrail, and climbed into the ring. She yanked Sherri away from Savage, hair first, and punched her, then she threw Sherri out of the ring and went to tend to the Macho Man" (Krebs 29).

A reconciliation between Savage and Elizabeth then was played out over several weeks. The subsequent marriage proposal took place at a Sacramento arena and was broadcast on the *WWF Wrestling Spotlight* (6 July 1991) in a brilliantly staged episode that was rebroadcast and elaborated upon repeatedly until the event itself. In the center ring, Mean Gene Okerlund held a microphone for Miss Elizabeth, who first affirmed her belief in marriage as a "sacred bond between a man and a woman" and then revealed her feelings for Randy Savage: "He's macho all right. But he's macho in a way I know him. He's warm, he's caring, he's affectionate . . . and, something a lot of people might not believe, he's very tender." Pointing to the announcer's table, where Savage was seated, she finished with "I just love that man." At this, Savage made his way to the ring. As a man in the audience shouted "on your knees!" he knelt and asked her to marry him. The camera then cut to images of women and girls in the audience wiping tears from their eyes and came to rest on a man and woman kissing before refocusing on the ring as Savage placed the ring on her finger, lifted her to his shoulder, and paraded with her around the ring. Billed as a "Match Made in Heaven," the wedding was performed live at *SummerSlam,* was broadcast live on pay-per-view, and was subsequently repackaged as part of the *SummerSlam '91* video for purchase by eager fans. Thus, the Macho Man's face turn was marked by a turning away from one kind of woman, the provocative and dangerous Scary Sherri, toward another, the sweetly, meekly feminine Miss Elizabeth. One representation of sexual union, outside the law and as such presumably perverse, was supplanted by another of the official variety, of the sort and in a manner that might be sanctioned by the entire community.[4]

Women can indeed turn from face to heel and vice versa, but because of the way in which they are positioned as consorts to male wrestlers their character shifts are generally more ambiguous. While Miss Elizabeth's demeanor did not change substantially over several years, she stood ringside first as a sign of Randy Savage's virtue, then became the destabilizing presence in the "Mega-Power" conflict between Savage and Hogan, and finally, still relatively unchanged, stood in the center of the ring as Savage was restored to grace via his marriage proposal to her. Similarly, Sherri may have turned face after a confrontation with her former associate Shawn Michaels, appearing unexpectedly against Michaels in Tatanka's corner at *Wrestlemania IX* at Caesar's Palace in 1993. But her essential persona—along with her makeup and style of dress—remained static.

Thus, when Savage and Hogan became allies and tag-team partners for a time, the breakdown of their male bond was provoked by a series of confrontations over Elizabeth in which Savage was seen to become increasingly irrational, progressively turning from face to heel as his clearly unjustified jealousy of the loyalty between Elizabeth and Hogan grew. But Miss Elizabeth's appearance of virtue was undamaged by Savage's attacks. Instead, she became a marker for his heel status, adding to his sins that of the man who abuses his loyal woman. At the same time, her presence at ringside was made visible as disruptive, nonetheless, both as the source of friction between the two men and as a distraction for Savage from the work of wrestling.

At the culminating confrontation, in *WrestleMania V*, Miss Elizabeth was interviewed for the pay-per-view broadcast before the match, where she professed her sorrow at the conflict between the two men and her own neutrality: "I only pray that neither man will be seriously injured" (2 April 1989). Escorted to ringside at Madison Square Garden, she was immediately confronted by Randy Savage pointing his finger and yelling fiercely at her, prompting face commentator Gorilla Monsoon to ask, with apparent naïveté, "Why does he keep bad-mouthing Miss Elizabeth?" To which Jesse "the Body" Ventura responded as the heel commentator: "She deserves it. She ought to be in his corner. He took her to the top." During the first part of the match, she displayed her anxiety with upturned face, trembling lips, and barely suppressed tears. Her attempts to succor the men as they took turns hitting the floor outside the ring placed her repeatedly between them until Savage chased her from the ring, grabbing her chin, pointing his finger, and shouting that she didn't belong. Sheltered by an official, she fled apparently in tears.

As a woman standing between two men, Miss Elizabeth came to represent a disruptive force and was marked as the catalyst for the degeneration of the idealized manly bond between Hulk Hogan and Randy Savage. While her character in performance actually changed little, and her hyperfeminine qualities remained intact, her presence at ringside was increasingly, irresistibly problematized. Face commentators Mean Gene Okerlund and Gorilla Monsoon sympathetically, albeit ineffectively, insisted on her position as victim, imagining her inner turmoil, while the heel commentator Jesse Ventura railed against Miss Elizabeth's meddling in particular and women in the ring in general. Gorilla repeatedly attempted to deflect Jesse's misogynist rants: "Devious? Not after the position she's been put in." Gene Okerlund gently began his interview with Elizabeth with "This has got to be the most difficult time of your entire life." Wishing her the best, he then turned back to the camera and solemnly announced that it was, indeed, "a very anxious moment for Miss Elizabeth." Jesse "the Body" Ventura, on the other hand, asserted: "What a gold-digger. . . . She's going to sit in a neutral corner . . . go with whoever wins." In the end, even Gorilla was forced to accept

Jesse's verdict that Miss Elizabeth was nothing more than "a trouble-maker" and to acknowledge that "Miss Elizabeth is causing all kinds of complications in this match." When she was finally ejected from ringside for distracting Savage, Gorilla was left without an effective rebuttal to Jesse's "Now we'll get down to *wrestling*. Get her out of the building. She never belonged in the first place."

For her part, when Sherri sided with Tatanka (the "Native American") against her former consort Shawn Michaels during *Wrestlemania IX* at Caesar's Palace in 1993, she never quite attained full face status. Despite obvious attempts to tone herself down—dressing in white, cutting down on the face paint, more or less silencing herself, looking up at the men from the floor, encouraging the hero with apparently genuine enthusiasm, preventing outside interference from giving Shawn Michaels an undue advantage—she remained a highly ambivalent, deeply disturbing figure, and was more jeered than cheered by fans. Another woman was introduced to perform the heel so that Sherri could play face in contrast. Luna Vachon in black leather and chains, full face paint, with wonderfully raspy *Hellraiser*-type snarls and screeches made energetic and often brilliant attempts at rule-breaking that seemed designed in large part to give Sherri the opportunity to play rule-enforcer. But although Sherri defended Tatanka and kept the match as straight as possible, and even went so far as to play the victim to Luna's vicious attack, the crowd's antipathy toward her seemed undiminished.

Moreover, Tatanka's evident unease at having Sherri in his corner was highly visible throughout the match. When, in a coda to the match, Luna ambushed Sherri, then clotheslined, kicked, and pummeled her into seeming half-consciousness, and left her prostrate on the ground outside the ring, Tatanka appeared compelled, as a gentlemanly man, to give succor to Sherri. Yet his expressions of outrage at the injustice done to Sherri, his visible care of her as he helped her to her feet never quite transcended an impression of his own distaste at being brought so close to her. Indeed, the best thing said about her, by Randy Savage acting as a face commentator, during the match served to reiterate her ambivalent status as a woman in a man's arena: "Wouldn't it be something if Sherri beat Shawn Michaels, and *she* was the Intercontinental Champion?"

The insistence that the ethic of the ring supersedes gender is always tenuously balanced against the evidence of hostility toward, coupled with a pornographic undercurrent to, any female presence in the arena. As with other aspects of wrestling, fans and wrestlers alike tend to introject their own ideals and ideologies into their readings of pro wrestling events and characters. A recent posting to the rec.sport.pro-wrestling newsgroup by a female fan reflects the wrestling world's conventional wisdom about gender while also echoing Sky Magic's ambivalently feminist stance:

> But I have to disagree with the complaints about the way women in the promotions are used. Francine has been trained as a wrestler. She is as tough as any guy in the ring. She is there of her own free will, and is not being forced to perform, or exploited (other than her body being exposed). She is a great heel. To say that she, a trained wrestler and performer, should not be an active part of the promotion, is sexist. I don't know if Beulah has been trained, but I assume she has been, because she can also give as good as she gets. IMO, they and Sherri Martel are the best example [sic] of the valet in the sport. I also like Woman. She is strong and sexy, but sexual in an active aggressive way, not as an object. I have a much bigger problem with the way McMahon uses Sunny in his promotion. She is nothing but a live pin-up, and is represented as having little or no intelligence. Same with Mrs. Mongo, but to a lesser degree, because she isn't being pushed as an object of sexual fantasy, but as one of ridicule. (Carrington 12 December 1996)

Along with many other wrestling participants, and women in particular, this female fan reconstructs the role of women in wrestling along the lines of a feminist ideal. From the wrestling event's available representations of women, they appear to cull positive female role models in resistance to what is obviously intended in the actual presentation. She admires women who are heels because they act in ways that appear powerful and empowering. However, what she ultimately acknowledges are the categorical readings of, and limitations on, women's performances. Woman, who is "sexual in an active aggressive way," along with Francine and Sherri, who give as good as they get, are effectively cast as dangerous women, heels; Sunny and Mrs. Mongo are rendered "impotent" by virtue of their parodic or hyperfemininity, faces who are no less intrusive for being objectified.

Women as wrestlers, managers, and spectators may act as the men do according to the game's masculine protocols, but what they represent in the arena is invariably linked to, and expressive of, their not being men, to their not-man-ness. Even if contained by representations of love and marriage, like Miss Elizabeth, or through other representations of sub-mission, as in the "rude awakening," a woman in the ring sooner or later comes into conflict with the male wrestlers and the idea(l) of masculine order. Like Scary Sherri, or even Miss Elizabeth in coming between the MegaPowers, a woman in the ring is inevitably a transgressor who de-serves what she gets and must take it "like a man" or get out.

In the WCW in 1991 manager Missy Hyatt came up against commenta-tor (and wrestler/promoter) Paul E. Dangerously and, consequently, challenged him to a bout. His response was to the point, echoing the basic ethic of the ring: "Missy will put herself in a man's place and be treated like a man" (*WCW Pro Wrestling* 22 June 1991). On a subsequent broadcast, he added: "I'm challenging a man. She's really a cross-dresser" (*WCW Pro Wrestling* 6 July 1991). Beyond asserting that she deserves the beating he will deliver, Dangerously's rhetoric held Missy to the between place of the woman who chooses to cross into masculine territory: simultaneously a transgressive figure who will learn her lesson the hard way and an opponent who will be treated as any other. That is, Missy might fight like a man, but she can never be one, and her challenge to Dangerously is an opportunity both to put her back into her place as a woman and to assert his own masculinity in contrast.

In this light it is perhaps not surprising that women wrestlers are most in evidence not in live events or in the televised broadcasts of the major circuits but on videos primarily advertised in wrestling magazines and available by mail order. Predictably, these videos are most often pre-sented in ways that approximate soft- or even hard-core pornography and, as a result, have little to do with wrestling per se, although unlike advertisements for homoerotic videos they are advertised in virtually all fan magazines. Titles such as "The Fierce World of Women Fighting" offer matches like that of "Peper [sic] vs. Salt" in which the buyer is promised the following (presumably interracial) spectacle: "Elsa and Vanessa struggle on the ropes and under the ropes, as well as all over the ring. A dominant hold earns a submission leaving the loser sweating and panting. In the second match bodies are pounded on the mat, and strain-ing muscles accentuate the perfect porportions [sic] of both bodies" (*Wrestling's Main Event,* September 1991, p. 51). One ad captioned "Beauty and Brutality" promises the buyer "Dresses, skirts, b[l]ouses ripped" with the tease: "Pull your chair close to the screen and feel the heat!" (*Wrestling Eye,* August 1991, p. 10).

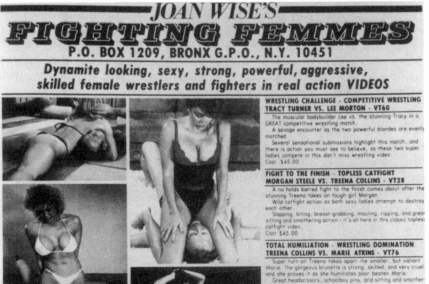

"FIGHTING FEMMES" (Advertisement from *Wrestling Eye*, August 1991)

Even the less overtly pornographic videos, those that feature women wrestlers who, at least superficially, perform according to the same rules as the men, walk the line between the spectacle of wrestling per se and pornographic display as the following examples from *The Best of Women's Championship Wrestling*[5] (or WCW, not the Turner Enterprise) and from a video produced by the Gorgeous Ladies of Wrestling (well-known as GLOW) amply demonstrate.[6] Both videos were taped at casinos whose logos feature prominently in many of the shots, and close with promotions for other videotapes as well as for magazines and fan clubs. In one ad, the WCW announcer promises, "You'll love corresponding with the totally hot girls of the WCW—a privilege only members may enjoy" along with "glamour, action, excitement," with the warning that "WCW battling beauties are waiting to hear from you—don't miss out!" As in men's wrestling, the American flag is displayed, but in the GLOW video the floor and ropes are pink, and chaser lights around the ring's base flash at the beginning and end of each match. The women wrestle under names like "Jail Bait," "California Doll," "Spanish Red," "Candi Divine," and "Lady Satan"—a veritable lineup of hooker-inflected monikers—and as with other female wrestlers, they are most often referred to simply as "the girls." Unlike men's wrestling, the women's performance is underscored by a loud musical background. The audience is small, largely but not solely male. Announcers in the ring and on the air are male, as are the referees and most of the managers, and the off-camera production crew as listed in the credits is predominantly male.

The GLOW video begins with close-up images of women, hair fluffed, lips moist, issuing their challenges straight into the soft-focused lens of the camera. These challenges are thinly veiled sexual come-ons at best: "I'm into necks. I like to get my strong arms around some girl's weak little pencil neck and squeeze the life out of her." "I'm 100 percent woman, but I wrestle like an animal, and I belong in there because I'm an animal. What do you think?" "I love to eat. Anything I can get my mouth on." A music video sequence follows in which images of women wrestling are collaged as Matilda the Hun sings a rap song with the refrain: "I eat raw meat." Interspersed between matches and at the video's end are more close-ups with more direct contact with the camera's eye and more direct sexual come-ons: "Get to know the real me. I can be real intimate." "I like a man you can have a little control over." "They need to satisfy me."

Even in the examples provided by GLOW and WCW, women wrestling look like men wrestling. The moves are the same, even the physical and verbal posturings are eerily consistent. But it seems impossible that they will ever be mistaken for anything other than "girls," "gorgeous ladies," or, taken one at a time "woman" with all it implies. What changes when women enter the squared circle is the relationship of the performer to the audience, as framed by the narratives provided by male announcers and cameramen, and by the habit, inculcated in the culture at large, of looking at women's performances as pornographic display. While men wrestling may be seen as a representation and, in many cases, mockery of homoerotic tensions in the culture, both in videos and in live performances, the spectacle of women wrestling may be seen to imitate male-generated pornographic images of pseudolesbian lovemaking. Men perform for their own and each other's pleasure, which may or may not include the pleasure of posing for, and demanding the desire of, women. Women's performances are never simply for each other, never outside the frame of the masculine, and always, at least implicitly, set within the context of (hetero)sexual provocation and promise.

In this context, even the most simple hold is transformed. No longer the expression of one man's power over another, when performed by a women a hold puts one woman in collusion with the male spectators by sustaining the exposure of the other's breasts or buttocks. The basic "cover" in which one wrestler pins another, generally by pulling a leg into the air, may be seen within the frame of dominance and submission when performed by men. When performed by women it becomes the means by which the women is "opened" for inspection for an extended, counted period of time. Similarly, when two men take hold of an opponent's legs in a split and pull him into the corner post, we are meant to wince in shared pain, a response the commentators often voice for the spectators. When the same move is performed by women, a distinctly different effect comes to mind.

The relationship of wrestler to authority and boundaries remains the same for both men and women. The referee is as frequently challenged, overridden, and assaulted by women as by men. The ropes form only a flimsy barrier to be crossed as often by women as men. And a brawl is just as much the highlight of the evening when women pour into the arena and over the ropes as when men do. But when women challenge the authority of the referee and the boundaries of the game, the act is less that of a shared revel and more effectively an unleashing that threatens to destabilize the entire event—as in the GLOW tape when the announcer calls for security and the video closes with the image of Matilda the Hun pushing him against the ropes, threatening further violation.

After even a quick survey of what's for sale, it is impossible to view women wrestling—in the match at Gleason's between Misty Blue and Linda Dallas, for example, or in Sky Magic's "professional" activities— outside the context of pornographic display. Professional wrestling's emphasis on the display of the body may be equally problematic for male wrestlers as well as for female wrestlers. But the compensatory strategies that are available to men are not equally available to women. The man's performance always leads attention from his body toward the spectacle of the contest: the fight. The woman's performance always returns the gaze to the display of her body. That is, the conventions by which performances of both men and women in wrestling are presented to be read by the audience remain essentially essentialist: in the end, the point is that this is a man and that is a woman.

Sky's successful marketing of herself as a wrestler has led to the presence of other women in the wrestlers' ring at Gleason's, albeit without the same commitment to ongoing training and drive toward professionalism. In one of her biggest coups, Sky was responsible for organizing a number of female bodybuilders to star with her in a girl wrestler video, which was to be the first step toward a whole girl wrestler cable/video industry. The company materialized in the ring one hot August day for a bit of training and choreography (21 August 1993). The producer/directors, Steve and Mitch, scrawny young men in shorts, sneakers, and ban-

Deb and Sarah try some wrestling moves. Boxers watch from ringside.

Deb chokes Sarah. The boxers watch.

dannas, were evidently new both to filmmaking and to wrestling. The women, Sarah and Deb, were Sky's acquaintances from her days on the bodybuilding circuit. The wrestlers, especially Chris, were both displaced from the ring and co-opted as coaches for a number of Saturday afternoons. The objective was not to make wrestlers of the girls per se, but to give them enough moves and confidence for the video to appear "real"—an almost impossible task as it turned out.

The work of introducing the new girls to the basic moves and holds was seriously undertaken by the wrestlers, who, from their seats next to me in my usual corner, alternately offered suggestions to Chris as he took the lead in coaching, hopped into the ring to demonstrate, and evaluated their progress. The girls, too, appeared quite serious, albeit visibly frustrated in their attempts to compress several months' worth of lessons into the one session and fearful of looking foolish as a result. The directors, perched precariously on the turnbuckles, appeared to be imitating both wrestler culture and Hollywood as they framed the girls with their hands in cliché moviemaking style and shouted instructions: "Show her your contempt, Deb!" "Strut your stuff, Sky!" "More attitude, girls!"

"You're proud of those muscles, show her . . . " The whole spectacle was avidly watched by every other man in the gym. Indeed, the moment the women took to the ring, the boxers, who ordinarily ignored the wrestlers except for occasional exchanges in passing, immediately abandoned their own workouts to hang at ringside opposite the wrestlers and me, offering their own sometimes barely obscured obscene commentaries to the girls and each other. The women were, in fact, beautifully fit, muscular, and graceful, and after the final training session the wrestlers urged Deb in particular to consider further training and the possibility of a real career. But in the context of the men directing and watching, the effect was embarrassing at best, and profoundly disturbing at moments.

The putative filmmakers having made themselves both unapproachable and ridiculous in their posturing, I turned to Sky to ask what the market would be for the girl wrestler video, how and to whom the thing would be distributed. As with our discussion about phone wrestling, her answers seemed to avoid what I thought was obvious: the connection between girl wrestling videos and soft-core porn. Instead, she told me that she'd been approached by some German producers about the possibility of touring Europe in a show to be called "Steel Cats" that would present girl wrestling in a context much like the Cirque du Soleil. She was somewhat skeptical of the legitimacy of the offer, and she said Sarah was worried about "white slavery." But they were taking the offer seriously, considering the possibilities for profit and stardom. When she stopped appearing at the gym a few months later, I initially assumed that she had decided to take the offer as another possible step up in her career as a professional wrestler. Ironically, I learn much later that Sky had moved on from wrestling to boxing, having decided that wrestling wasn't "masculine" enough (DeGaris, e-mail correspondence 24 January 1997).

Chapter Six

"REAL" LIFE

I'll ask you the standard question.

—John Stossel

Why do people believe in a bunch of actors that get together
and play fight? These guys are nothing but actors that act
mad at each other and call each other names and then pre-
tend to beat each others [sic] heads in. Then after the so
called match they go to the bar together and drink beer and
laugh at all the money that they made off a bunch of fools
that believed they were actually fighting. Beats me. Get it?

—anonymous RSPW poster (19 December 1996)

I don't care if it's real or not. Kill him! Kill him!

—a fan, any fan

The fans believe—and the 'rasslers do too. But you don't
want to know about that. All you want is the answer to one
question: Is 'rassling real? Did he really hit you? And the
answer is: I know, but you don't know. The answer is: What
do you mean by real?

—Clifton Jolley

"So. What do you think? You think wrestling's fake?" I'm being
tested once again (2 August 1993). This time it's Rubio, although almost every wrestler has thrown the question at me
in some way. I answer him as I've answered the others: "If by 'fake' you
mean do I think the game is fixed, and 'real' means that it's supposed to
be a *contest*, then wrestling's a fake. But if you're asking me if I think you
guys are really strong, really skilled, really athletic, then it's real. That

makes it real to me. And I also think you guys have to be very smart, really know what you're doing, or you'll kill each other and yourselves." Satisfied, he goes back to working out. Relieved, I go back to watching, taking photographs and notes.

A couple of months later (17 April 1993), when I arrive at Gleason's the first thing I see is Rubio in the ring "wrestling" with a young boy, who appears to be the son of one of the boxers and, at about three and a half feet tall, looks about nine or ten years old. Standing somewhat shyly in the ring and cheerfully encouraged by Rubio and Frankie, the boy pushes Rubio with a finger, causing Rubio to perform an extraordinary series of pratfalls, landing prone and panting at the boy's feet in an exaggerated display of submission. At the end of the display, Rubio issues the first of what were to be regular invitations to me: I, too, can get into the ring with him and win a few rounds.

But I don't get in the ring. And I don't tell the wrestlers that what they do is fake. No boxed ears for me. I'm not John Stossel, the *20/20* reporter who in his relentless "exposé" of pro wrestling was senseless

Rubio and Frankie working out. The precision of Lucha Libre extends
to their fingertips.

Rubio and Frankie working together to create a new sequence of moves.

enough, even after what must have been at least a few weeks of researching and filming wrestlers, to pose the "standard question" to an obviously hostile David "Dr. D." Schultz outside the ring, and who suffered
a very real beating as a result.

> Stossel: "I'll ask you the standard question."
> Schultz: "Standard question?"
> Stossel: "I think it's fake . . ."
> Schultz: "You think it's fake, huh?" (Slaps Stossel on each ear with an
> open hand, then as Stossel falls, kicks and taunts the fleeing reporter.)

No, indeed. If nothing else, I'm well aware of the wrestlers' potential for
actual violence when confronted with an outsider's skepticism. By the
time I'm being asked the wrestler's version of the "standard question,"
I'm more like Clifton Jolley, who comes to be "in on the game"—or at
least to sound as though he's "in on the game"—in his PBS special on
professional wrestling, *I Remember Gorgeous George.* Like Jolley, I have
come "inside" insofar as this is possible given that, unlike Jolley, I resist
entering the ring myself. Like Jolley, I have come to recognize what
many fans accept: that what they watch when they watch professional
wrestling is not what they watch when they watch other sporting events
and, consequently, that the question of real versus fake is not quite the
point.

Paradoxically, while the popular press almost invariably focuses on
and criticizes professional wrestling's fakery, scholarly writing almost
always reduces the meanings produced by wrestling to its morality play
aspects. Yet what must be recognized is that in order to control and shape
the play of virtue and vice to a moral end, the game *must* be fixed. How,
then, are we to reconcile the clichés of childhood sportsmanship—"It's
not whether you win or lose; it's how you play the game"—with the
transparent unfairness of wrestling: that it's not a fair fight on any level,
that if it's not that the bad guy has cheated, then it's that the promoter
has fixed the finish? Roland Barthes closes his seminal essay with a paean
to an idea of professional wrestling's moral certainties, in which he
exults:

> A wrestler can irritate or disgust, he never disappoints, for he always
> accomplishes completely, by a progressive solidification of signs, what
> the public expects of him. In wrestling, nothing exists except in the
> absolute, there is no symbol, no allusion, everything is presented ex-

haustively. Leaving nothing in the shade, each action discards all para-
sitic meanings and ceremonially offers to the public a pure and full
signification, rounded like Nature. This grandiloquence is nothing but
the popular and age-old image of the perfect intelligibility of reality.
What is portrayed by wrestling is therefore an ideal understanding of
things; it is the euphoria of men raised for a while above the constitu-
tive ambiguity of everyday situations and placed before the panoramic
view of a univocal Nature, in which signs at last correspond to causes,
without obstacle, without evasion, without contradiction. (25)

Yet, the apparent moral clarity of wrestling is not so clear after all. Professional wrestling's moral universe is, in fact, imbued with essential contradictions within and between the fiction of the play and the fact of the
business. What fans come to recognize and interact with as they come
inside the game is the play outside the play: first the signs of a hero or
villain, then the inevitable failure of the representatives of authority in
the ring to assure a fair fight and a just end, and finally that the true
power lies not in the ring at all but rather in the hands of the promoter
whose purchase of a wrestler includes the right to dictate his success or
failure.

What is certain is not a "Justice which is at last intelligible" (Barthes
25) but an *Injustice* which is visible both in the dramaturgy of the performance and in the structure of the game itself, in the ongoing failure
of authority to assert itself for the hero in the ring and in the success of
the authority outside the ring, the promoter, as he dictates an outcome
that negates the possibility of any genuine contest between men. It is not
a fair fight, neither for the wrestlers in the ring, nor for the wrestlers and
the fans in relation to those in power. The microcosm of the squared
circle reflects first the largely unseen conditions of the game and then
the world outside. As in the game that is wrestling, the game of life, at
least its finish, is almost certainly fixed.

But if what fans are being told by the performance is that they don't
stand a chance against those who are more economically and hierarchi-
cally powerful in the culture—the owners, the bosses, the lawyers, the
politicians—why is professional wrestling so popular? Why would the
fans return to arenas and their televisions with such devotion if what
they are being sold is simply the representation of futility, of their own
potential losses and actual disempowerment as workers and as consumers? Where is the satisfaction in witnessing repeated demonstrations of

the failure of those who represent truth, justice, and the American way—the hero, the rules, the referee, the ropes—to prevail against lies, unfairness, and more than a few corrupt foreign bodies?

As with everything else in professional wrestling, the truth lies somehow with the cheat. When I first started this research in 1989, in my naïveté, before I'd read Barthes or consulted the relatively small body of scholarly writing on wrestling, I did three things: I watched television, went to matches, and found my way to the wrestlers' gym. In the first two actions, I sat with the fans; in the latter, I sat with would-be and working professional wrestlers. What astonished me then, what amazes me still is the enthusiasm with which fans actively claim their knowledge and authority, their rightness and righteousness as participants in the professional wrestling event, even as they rail against this wrestler or that promoter. They don't simply cheer or jeer, celebrate or lament as their favorites win or lose. They narrate the event, anticipate a turn or a finish, evaluate the performance as a performance. They tell each other, and anyone who will listen, the background of each wrestler: his current story line, his wrestling history, and the details of his "real" life, his name, his marital status, his original occupation, his wrestling patri-lineage, and so on. They wax nostalgic for the good years of wrestling—the fifties and sixties for some, the eighties now for others—and complain about the cynicism of the promoters, the way in which the event we are witnessing is no longer "real" wrestling but ersatz, a cheap counterfeit. They wouldn't buy the ticket, the pay-per-view, the magazine, the souvenir, if it were not for liking this particular wrestler or wanting to see that particular angle played out.

At Madison Square Garden, at Gleason's Arena, at countless arenas and venues around the United States and the world . . . The action slows in the ring for a moment, becomes repetitive, static. The fans stand together and take up the chant: "Bor-ring!" In response, the wrestlers immediately accelerate: a wrestler bodyslams his opponent and then catapults from the top rope, and/or they take it out of the ring and into the front rows, and/or a couple of stars race from the locker room to mix things up in the ring. Satisfied that they've been heard, the fans settle back into their seats. Everything about the event, from the advance publicity—the development of grudges into angles and story lines culminating in the announcement of the evening's card—to the action in the ring, has explicitly catered directly to them. The promoter promises: he's going to give them what they want, "real" wrestling. If it happens that what the promoter presents fails to fulfill their expectations, the fans have ways of telling him and his wrestlers so. It is a consumer's paradise, no deception here. They've been promised their money's worth, and if they are rarely fully satisfied, they remain optimistic enough to return on a regular basis—in the tens of thousands to live matches, in the millions to weekly programs and pay-per-views—for more of the same. Asked if they think it's real or fake, most fans prevaricate as much as the wrestlers. Even the neophytes, except for the youngest children, will acknowledge at least having heard that the game is fixed, that wrestlers don't really land all those punches, that the moves are choreographed. . . .

John Stossel begins his now infamous *20/20* report (1 February 1985) on the perfidy of pro wrestling by recognizing that "apparently, *this* is what the public wants." He displays his moral outrage: "This stuff kind of makes me mad, because this isn't really wrestling. This is *'rassling.*" He goes on: "I was a high school wrestler. *That's* wrestling. *I* appreciate it, but that's because *I* understand the sport." With this he establishes his credentials; he is a wrestling connoisseur who knows the difference

Larry hits Chris, or does he? Tommy watches.

Chris attempts to regain his composure. Mohammed and Johnny
watch from ringside.

between the fake and the real. Doing "what any journalist would do" in pursuit of the truth, he takes an "exit poll," talking to fans under the "EXIT" sign after a WWF match at Madison Square Garden where he gets the predictable range of responses: "I think it's all fake, you know. It's a form of entertainment," one man declares. "Well, it's fun, but it's fake," a boy says, adding, "I mean, they don't hit 'em in the head and everything and make 'em bleed and everything." The women in Stossel's poll seem more gullible: "I don't think a lot of people are gonna pay their money to come see a play fight out there," one asserts. Another simply states, "No, I don't think it's fixed. No, baby." Still trolling for an answer, he goes "backstage" and "the Iron Sheik" (Ali Vazarri) a ring veteran who gives the same challenge-in-response I've heard from Johnny and the others: "Come in the ring. I can take your head off. Or anybody else's. My sport is not phony. Come in the ring. I show you. Anything else?"[1] Then, Stossel announces in all (apparent) seriousness: "But, fans, I'm afraid I have to tell you. (Pause.) It *is* fake."

He continues his pursuit of the inside scoop, exposing Vince McMa-

Tommy steps into a fight.

hon ("the man in the vest") with all the expressive earnestness of a contemporary Dorothy seeing the real Wizard of Oz behind the curtain for the first time. He uncovers and shows us the tricks, the way wrestlers work with rather than against each other and the blading, by stepping into the ring with a disgruntled ex-wrestler. He listens attentively to another ex-wrestler who claims he quit because of homosexual coercion and to a female promoter who has been squeezed out of the Atlanta market. Stossel's ultimate targets are not the hardworking wrestlers but the promoters, who are revealed to abuse their wrestlers and create monopolies, implicitly implicating Vince McMahon in particular. His report closes with the confrontation with David Schultz and the danger that fake violence can become real. In a coda Barbara Walters commiserates with Stossel, who (it appears) has suffered serious permanent damage to his ears, and tells the viewing audience: "I hope that nobody thinks that this was part of your story. You really *were* beaten by this man." Ruefully, he tells her of his journalistic prowess, pursuing all kinds of crooks and fakers, but "the one time I get hit is when it's obvious that it's a fake." Walters recaps Stossel's story, calling it "amazing": "It started out being funny and entertaining, then became very real . . . *too* real, in your case."

What becomes apparent in this exposé is the convergence of two not dissimilar narratives. The *20/20* program can be read as a morality play that is no less codified and reductive than that of professional wrestling as presented within the program. Characters and action conform to the dramaturgical conventions of investigative journalism, and, like wrestling, its presentation of a contest between virtue and vice even includes a high degree of gender stereotyping (the "smart" male fans in contrast to the "mark" female fans) as well as archetypal characterizations (the noble and beleaguered underdogs versus the imperious bosses). In the end, the assumption of a patriotic, masculine ideal remains unquestioned and the outcome is as expected: Wrestling is a fake, and its economics pose a danger to the American ethos. It even has a final twist, a bit of genuine heat, real violence and real blood, in its last minutes. The intrepid reporter, call him "Little John," self-consciously presents himself to his audience as virtuous if a bit naive in his faith in the rules of sportsmanlike conduct. He even talks directly to his audience, assuming their collusion in his quest, before he boldly (and literally) steps into the ring to do battle with a threat to the American community's ethical foundations. Everyone knows that it's his job to ask these questions. He's the one who gets to throw the (verbal) punches. He's the American journalist standing for freedom of the press and the American way. The renegade wrestler—"most are just hardworking guys who know it's a fake"—transgresses the boundaries of proper interviewee behavior. As he attacks the hero "for real," outside the ring, in the context of the interview, David Schultz then stands in for and becomes a symbol of the corruption that the wrestling audience doesn't necessarily see and wouldn't necessarily recognize if actual blood were not drawn as proof.

The moral of the *20/20* story is that the "fake" violence of the performance not only leads to "real" violence but, more important, is symptomatic of the "real" dangers of wrestling's dishonesty. The cheat of the wrestling performance and the promoters' corruption, it is implied, may overflow the boundaries and infect American society "for real." Implicit in Walters's attempt to assert the "reality" of what happened to Stossel is a fear that, with the exposure of wrestling's fraudulent representational ethos, the viewer's perception of authenticity of the *20/20* program will itself be destabilized. That is, as Walters insists that Stossel's narrative is not "part of [the] story" she (I assume inadvertently) points toward her own anxiety. Paradoxically, the notion that "fake" violence might be-

come "real" and leak from the wrestling event into life implies the possibility of another kind of leakage. One revelation of simulation implies
the probability of others, even by those who are doing the revealing. If
wrestling is fake, a contrived performance scripted in order to manipulate gullible spectators and thereby increase the promoters' profits, as
Stossel demonstrates, then what is to prevent the *20/20* audience from
viewing Stossel's confrontation with Schultz as staged on the same terms
and for the same reasons? What Walters and Stossel tiptoe around in
the end is what many hard-core wrestling fans would see as the point:
everything—wrestling, life, the whole shooting match—might really be
a work.

For the fans, not only are the stories that are told to them in the
ongoing professional wrestling narratives drawn from life, life itself can
be read through the structures and understandings that professional
wrestling provides. Current events become material for characters and
stories, as one fan announces to the RSPW newsgroup, presumably with
irony intended: "Harry Helmsley, who was husband of the target of sat-
ire [Leona] for Vince [McMahon], died yesterday. There as been no word
from Titan as to whether they will make an angle out of his death" (Sheir
6 January 1997). Conversely, a recent discussion on RSPW quickly
moves beyond why current WWF champion Bret Hart cannot be a Republican (he's Canadian) to reconstituting the current political scene as
a wrestling angle. The original poster begins the shift with "Anyway, I
apologize for bringing this political BS into this NG and I won't mention
it again unless Gingrich signs to meet Clinton in a cage at Wrestlemania
13" (Smith 31 December 1996). Another puns: "What about mad dog
dornan against bill clinton in a fallsa count anywhere match at the next
starcade :-)" (Haller 3 January 1997). Another implies that political
events are generally contrived much as wrestling events and that the
plots are not dissimilar: "After Dornan gave that shoot interview about
the Evil Mexicans taking over Southern California, I don't think he'll
ever be hired by a major US promotion again" (Grant 3 January 1997).
Pointing to the power of negative heat, another proposes an angle: "The
heat-generating power of the 'B-1 Bob' gimmick cannot be denied, so
there's ALWAYS going to be a place for him in a major promotion, in spite
of the difficulties. Consider the possibilities of bitter war veteran B-1
Bob teaming with Mr. Bob Backlund to instill respect and morality in
America's youth. Better yet, imagine B-1 being seconded at Wrestlema-

nia or Starrcade [sic] by his old friend, the 'Monster from Missouri,' [popular neo-conservative talk-radio host] Rush H. Limbaugh III" (Unsigned 3 January 1997).

To know the rules by which the game of wrestling is played, not just the names of the moves but the way the wrestling event is constructed by promoters, is to know how the game of life is played. Whether in the arena or in the magazines and on the 'net, fans love to display their expertise. They are "smarts" not "marks." As what Henry Jenkins has termed "textual poachers," they not only compete against one another in spotting the fix and predicting the angle, they construct narratives of their own, from conceiving of politics as wrestling to fantasy wrestling networks. Jenkins notes the sophistication of fan culture, calling it "an institution of theory and criticism, a semistructured space where competing interpretations and evaluations of common texts are proposed, debated, and negotiated and where readers speculate about the nature of the mass media and their own relationship to it" (86). Against the assumption that theoretical and critical activity is the exclusive domain of the academic, Jenkins declares that fans are the "true experts" of popular culture, constituting "a competing educational elite, albeit one without official recognition or social power" (86). What is important and empowering to wrestling fans, then, what they repeatedly seek to display and prove is their hard-won knowledge of the game, their facility with its vocabulary and dramaturgy, and their position in the exchange.

Professional wrestling's fan culture is extraordinarily rich and complex, with many regular spectators also distributing their own newsletters (on paper and on the 'net) as well as getting involved at least peripherally in staging matches. One such fan/participant is Ben Lagerstrom, a.k.a. "Big Daddy Money Bucks" and "the Shoeshine Boy." In our first conversation he told me of his obsessive love of the game: "Ever since I was six years old it's been my dream to be in the wrestling business" (phone conversation 20 July 1994). When we met in person, what I saw was a tall, soft-appearing (although not overweight) fifteen-year-old, wearing glasses, with wisps of beard and mustache matched by a ponytail. He told me of his wrestling archives—more than six hundred videotapes, newsletters, and magazines—and that he was also publishing his own newsletter ("The Squared Circle") and managing a couple of wrestlers in a small local promotion (interview 1994). Ben was full of ambition. His plans included a two-week excursion to Seattle, Washington, where he said he had a friend with a connection who might find him wrestling work. He also talked of a possible trip to Japan and of hustling tours to Puerto Rico and London. Most of all, he was proud of an appearance on the WWF's *Monday Night RAW*, in which he shined the Million Dollar Man Ted DiBiase's shoes and which had earned him the name "Shoeshine Boy." He was riding on this moment of fame in his local gigs, where he would appear as heel manager "Big Daddy Money Bucks" and dare the audience to call him "Shoeshine Boy," which of course, he said, they did with great glee.

Clearly intelligent and obviously privileged—in particular, being "home-schooled" gave him room to pursue his dream—Ben considered himself no longer a fan or a mark but an insider: "I can give you Vince McMahon's phone number, but don't tell him it was me." Eager to set himself apart from the fans, he talked about working as a ring boy for the ECW in Philadelphia where he blamed unruly fans for creating an uncontrolled situation. Eager to demonstrate his "smarts," he displayed his vocabulary and taught me a few new words, described the day-to-day existence of most wrestlers, and shared gossip about drug use in the big leagues, telling me that most promoters won't tolerate steroids because they cause wrestlers to "fuck up their spots," but that many wrestlers (whose names he was pleased to share with me) are on other drugs. Eager to legitimize himself as a manager, he showed me his promotional materials. And eager to distinguish himself and claim his authority over my other sources, he pooh-poohed the training at Gleason's, telling me that that the ring wasn't authentic ("a boxer's ring with no spring"), that Johnny "teaches a few bumps" but not wrestling and that his wrestlers don't work at all ("don't get a payday"). While at the time I found myself surprisingly defensive on Johnny's behalf—the ring is a real wrestler's ring, the wrestlers do work—in retrospect, it was an astonishing display of desire, of genuine fanaticism: nine years of watching at ringside, dreaming of being in on the game with just enough of a toehold (and little enough parental restraint) to sustain his urgency.

Everyone who comes into contact with wrestling—from the first time spectator to the most experienced wrestler or promoter, even the occasional academic—is engaged in a process of coming inside. Beyond knowing that the finish is fixed, the more hard-core the fan, the more he or she is knowledgeable about the way in which matches are constructed and promoted. Like the wrestlers, they insist on respect for, and the

integrity of, the game: "Just because the finishes of wrestling are prede-
termined and have been since the beginning of this century doesn't mean
that laws and ethics do not apply to those involved in this business."[2]
With a knowledge and ferocity that would impress any theatre producer
or teacher, they argue about the believability of characters and evaluate
story lines, talking back to promoters in the arena as well as in their own
networks: "Hey Eric [Bischoff, WCW promoter] . . . psssst . . . I've got a
word for you . . . It's called CATHARSIS. That basically means that all
your angles should have an ENDING! Try it sometime. At least McMahon
[WWF promoter], with his limited roster and gimmicks for 12-year-olds,
knows when to end a story" (Unsigned 31 December 1996).

They note the shifts in dramaturgical practice—for example, from
clarity to ambiguity in the positioning of wrestlers, weighing the pros
and cons. One RSPW fan begins with a question: "Someone please help
me out with this Michaels/Hart angle [WWF]. Bret is supposed to be the
face, right? And Michaels is supposed to be the tweener/heel right? So
why do they have Bret making excuses and whining and Michaels coming right out and admitting that he was beaten even though he is the
one who has the excuse?" He then goes on to evaluate the theatrical
implications for himself: "I'm not saying this is bad, for too long the
lines between faces and heels have been too clear cut in the WWF. Now,
thank goodness all the faces don't have to be friends, and all the heels
don't have to be friends, moreover, whether a lot of guys are heel or face
(Michaels, Bulldog, Hart, Goldust, Bret etc. etc.) is unclear, which is an
excellent step in the right direction, to increasing the realism. Having
Bret behaving true to [heel commentator] Lawler's 'Excellence of Excuses' [a pun on Bret's 'Excellence of Execution' refrain] label, is going
to put Michaels even more over than he is, which is great, because he's a
superb talent and deserves it. But at the expense of the Hitman? Why?"
(Mirza 6 January 1997).

Ultimately, the real contest from the fans' perspective is not between
wrestlers, with whom they identify, but rather between themselves as
competing experts and, most important, between the fans as consumers
and the promoters who produce and market the wrestling product. They
complain when certain wrestlers are "pushed" and others repeatedly
used as "jobbers," and they evaluate the heat generated by a particular
wrestler, gimmick, angle, or match, often proving their points by describing the "pop" from the other fans as they try to second-guess the

promoters. The basis for the contract between promoter and spectator is economic, a promise that fans will get their money's worth. It is perhaps ironic that the fans who might be considered fanatic addicts, those who spend the most time and money on wrestling, are the least passive purchasers. Rather they actively engage in recouping their investment in the ticket, the pay-per-view, the magazine and souvenir, often regarding their efforts as part of a natural struggle to win against the promoter, whose sole desire is, as one RSPW poster put it, to create "an empty void in your pockets!" (Councell 6 January 1997).

More than skeptical of the wrestling event as an elaborate con game, many fans are openly antagonistic toward promoters and proud of their facility for retrieving pleasure regardless of what is offered to them. For one fan, who calls himself "Superfan," the point is to remain autonomous, a "real" wrestling fan, unsold and unmarked by the promoter's guile: "Both [the WWF and the WCW] cheat their fans. That's the way of the promoter. At least the WCW gives us some great mid-card matches, while the WWF fills it full of Hog Farmers battling imposters from another promotion. I'm no WCW fan, I'm no WWF fan, I'm no ECW fan, I'm no international fan, I'm a wrestling fan. I take bits and pieces of all the promotions, and put together a wrestling reality that suits my interests best. I think that is what we all should do instead of saying on[e] is better than the other, although this is wrestling and that is the nature of the beast" (The Superfans 1 January 1997). For this fan, as for many others, knowing how that wrestling is fixed is liberating rather than constraining, a form of imaginative empowerment. To be in on the game as a fan offers the fan the potential for constructing and enjoying the wrestling performance on highly individualistic terms.

Hard-core fans are explicitly obsessed with reading live and televised wrestling performances for the signs of the real and the fake. But rather than looking for proof of the fix, what they seek is twofold: opportunities to demonstrate their expertise in reading (and explaining) performances and moments when the display of violence becomes, or at least appears to have become, actual. That is, the fans operate in a tension between wanting to appear "smart" and wanting the experience of the "mark," of what they call "marking out." In what might be considered an informed discussion of suspension of disbelief in which belief is never fully suspended, they debate, in their terms and on the basis of their knowledge of a wrestler's "true" history or their close observation of the event: "Was it a work, or a shoot?" The sign that the game has crossed from simulation to actuality is generally tied to the revelation of injury, for which blood is the most vivid sign. The knowledge that wrestlers blade their foreheads does not necessarily diminish the impact of seeing blood stream down a wrestler's face, and in any case, the fact that the bleeding may be self-induced does not make the blood itself less real, regardless. Aware of the actual risks involved in wrestling—the hazards of slamming, hitting, and leaping at another man—the fans are driven to look more closely, to look again, and to come back for another chance to look.

When Billy Gunn of the Smoking Gunns (WWF) is carried from the ring after being slammed by his "brother" Bart, one fan worries: "I couldn't sleep last night thinking that Billy could be seriously injured" (Malecki 18 December 1996). Another responds: "The only way he's hurt is if the dopes carrying the stretcher dropped him on the way out. Compared to Shawn's collapse (which had me fooled for the duration of the show at least), this was blatantly obvious. If they hadn't had one of their wives say 'How can you do this to your brother?' (even marks who've seen them before the WWF know they aren't even related), it might have worked a little bit. That line killed what little cred[ibility] that work had for me though" (Thompson 18 December 1996).

This thread peters out with an insult—"It's a work and if you can't see that you're more of a mark then [sic] I am" (Slugger 123 18 December 1996). But it leads directly into an extended debate over the facts of Shawn Michaels' injury. One fan asks: "I have a co-worker who thinks that the Shawn Michaels collapsed [sic] last year due to head injuries was real. However, I felt it was a work. As a matter of fact I'm 100% sure it was a fake. So can anyone tell us once and for all if it was a for real or a fake" (Chung 20 December 1996). He is told: "The head injuries (among others) were real, he was attacked, while out with Davey Boy Smith and 1-2-3 Kid Sean Waltman. The collapse on Raw was 100% staged, and the best work in wrestling history. Period" (Meisner 20 December 1996). This leads to further explanation: "Let me take it one step further and explain to Richard that, from what I could find out, the RAW collapse was faked BECAUSE of the real injuries sustained during the Syracuse attack. Because of very real injuries they created the angle in order to give Shawn a break. This fact alone makes the angle, in my opinion, more remarkable. It's amasing [sic] to me that they could come up with and execute such a realistic and believable angle in such a short time. I for one had already become rather jaded as far as angles go and for at least the moment that it was occurring, I was a believer" (Powerhug 22 December 1996). To which is added: "And it proves to everyone that the Michaels collapse was incredibly realistic, because it was based on resalistic [sic] events. I personally marked out huge, I was sweating bullets afterwards, and I was wondering where the hell I could find info on the collapse after. This was before RSPW. Tyson's opponents should have been taking notes" (Gokhale 22 December 1996). Clearly, from the perspective of at least one wrestling fan, boxers such as Peter MacNeeley would do well to learn how to perform a showstopping injury from the real pros.[3] While the fans' concern for the well-being of wrestlers is evident, what is striking is the way in which their desire to know the *truth* about injuries is constantly balanced against their evaluation of the *performance* of injuries.

Even fan behavior is suspect and comes under scrutiny, as when someone attempted to attack Rowdy Roddy Piper and Hulk Hogan in the ring during the main event at *Starcade* (WCW 1996): "Well the guy who charged the ring /had/ to be a shoot. I mean, did you see how strong the ref became when he started going after the fan? No wimpy pushover any more! I also notice that when a fan gets stomped at the edge of the ring (like at Bash at the Beach during Hogan's heel turn) the stomps are quieter since they're putting more weight on the stomping foot and less on the noisemaker foot" (Long 30 December 1996). This display of knowledge and observational skills leads to the ultimate put-down: "What marks! The fan at the Bash was a work and so was the one at Starcade. If a real fan rushed the ring, the wrestlers would probably run like heeck [sic] from him because the guy could have a gun! Ask any professional athlete what happens when a fan runs onto the field or into the ring. They usually let security handle it because they don't know what the guy has on him. This was so obviously a work that anybody who believed it was real probably thought the guy who got up in the ring and took a picture of Hogan with an exploding camera while he was in the WWF was also real" (Johnson 30 December 1996). This leads to an argument based on dramaturgy and business: "Don't be a moron. Are you telling me that [a]fter a month of non-stop barrage of ads for the 'match of the decade' that during the ending sequence, featuring Piper getting out of the chokeslam and slapping the sleeper on Hogan, that WCW would send in a plant to confuse the ending, distract the audience, and overall accomplish absolutely nothing. As for waiting for security, it was a good 6 or 7 seconds before the guards made it to the mark. Hogan would have been dead whether he intervened or not" (Horowitz 30 December 1996). The definitive answer seems to come from the eyewitness, who tells the others: "Well after Starrcade [sic] all of the hardcore fans went outside and cheered the fan as he went away in the paddy wagon. His face was real bloody and he was drunk off his ass. However, he was glad to hear our cheers . . . he may be a lowly loner with nothing else but wrestling, but hey, it was brave of him to do what he did. LONG LIVE THE DRUNK FAN!" (Unsigned 1 January 1997).

The play of the fake and the real can extend well beyond the fight and the presentation of wrestlers as characters. One *Monday Night RAW* episode remains a vivid reminder that at the center of the wrestling event is a celebration of performance as performance, the fake for its own sake.[4] It featured a much-reviled wrestler named Bastion Booger as a guest commentator at ringside. A grotesque, gray-bodied, and hairy five-hundred-pound monster, Booger's gimmick was simply and effectively to gross out the audience with whatever means were available to him. Often blowing snot directly from his nose at the audience and then at the camera was sufficient provocation to bring spectators to their feet. But he also would sexually taunt his opponents, who would exclaim and mime their disgust and reluctance to touch him in any way, even to wrestle. Booger made a tremendous display of eating his way through the performance: pizza, burgers, hot dogs, french fries, and god knows what else were delivered at brief intervals for him to shove into his mouth throughout the show. Periodically, the camera would zoom into close-up to show him mashing handfuls of food into and around his mouth, which he then opened, allowing the food to dribble out an obscene version of the children's game of "see-food" as Vince McMahon and the other commentators groaned in revulsion.

Bastion Booger eating was not a pretty sight. Or was it? The pièce de résistance, an oversized and lavishly overiced cake, was delivered, and Booger dug into it, smearing it liberally over himself and spitting mouthfuls onto the table with his gap-toothed, snot-dripping grin. But on looking again, both at my tape and the replays on other WWF programming, it was clear: Booger was only pretending to eat. What was performed and what we were told we were seeing was not, in fact, what we saw. As the commentators howled with disgust, what was fully visible throughout was that Booger was simply smearing food on himself, taking if anything, only small nibbles out of whatever was in his hands. For no apparent reason—it is hard to imagine this wrestler shying away from the gross or, for that matter being on a diet—except, perhaps, for the sheer pleasure of the con, Booger was making a performance where the real might have sufficed. He was faking it. Like any other fan, I first marked out and then went back for another, hard-core look. Far from being disappointed by what I discovered, I found that I was pleased, simultaneously proud of myself for seeing through a performance that had genuinely disturbed me and eager to uncover more such examples of fakery.

The more insistent fans become in their exposés of wrestling's fakery, the more they look to experience the real. As they expose the con artistry of the game, they revel in it and, on some level, seek to be conned, at least momentarily. They "see through" the fiction of the wrestling event to its facts, to distinguish between what is improvised and what is staged, between the real and the not-so-real event, and in so doing attempt to shatter any illusions others might have. Yet they also appear to yearn for the illusion to be real regardless. That is, they disbelieve what they see as they look to believe. Just as they are often nostalgic for the good old days of wrestling, they seem nostalgic for the time when they still believed the fictions presented. They revel in their own deception, and they discuss, sometimes rapturously, the moments when they "marked-out," when they were fooled into believing that the wrestler was injured for real, that the fan rushed the ring for real, that the blood was not from a blade but was for real, that the promoter's grip over the wrestlers and the matches will slip, that the fight will be more than play, and that they will see the violence for real. This phantom of the real is at the heart of professional wrestling's appeal. It keeps the fans coming back for another look, keeps them reading into and through performances and predicting future events for each other.

Paradoxically, what is fervently desired—the moment of real impact, the display of real blood—is also secretly dreaded. At a match at Gleason's Arena in 1989 the action slammed to a halt when a wrestler, one of the Twin Towers, was thrown from the ring onto the concrete. What had been a fast and furious tag-team match accompanied by raucous shouts from the audience went fully, deadly silent. The wrestlers, good guys and bad alike, froze. Spectators rushed to look over shoulders while the referee and judges checked out the nearly unconscious man. Everyone

A new wrestler bodyslams Mohammed.

waited until he arose and reentered the ring. The match resumed, with the Twin Towers winning the NCW tag-team title to the loud cheers of the crowd. But the blood on the concrete and the man's damp, matted hair remained vivid reminders of the very real risks to the game. The spectacle had collapsed into reality. And yet, as we left the arena, I overheard some debating whether or not the moment had been staged.

Given that most wrestlers begin as fans, it is not surprising that the wrestlers at Gleason's are no less captivated by the convergence of the real and the fake both in performances that they see and in their own workouts. In fact, on the day I began this research in 1989, I watched as one wrestler, Gino, was hurt when his opponent, a novice, shied away from a dropkick. The shift in the atmosphere was electric. The other wrestlers pushed Gino's sparring partner away and kept him at a distance for a good ten minutes while they examined Gino's injury and offered advice. Only after Gino had reassured the others that he would be okay was the other man allowed to approach and apologize. At the same time, one of the others confronted me with "Game, huh?!"

Years later, and several weeks after his confrontation with Tommy, I

Mohammed is flipped.

asked Larry whether or not he had been seriously fighting Tommy or was it still the game on some level (16 July 1994). He prevaricated a bit, then answered that he doesn't necessarily know himself when he's shooting and when he's working. He described a long-ago workout with Johnny during which he became increasingly uncertain about the nature of the sparring. It was off in some way, he said; they were grabbing each other, and the tension was building with each exchange. When they finished, he told me, they asked each other what had happened, but neither of them was sure of the answer.

What is "real" wrestling? Even as they disparage the critics who say that professional wrestling isn't "real" wrestling, the wrestlers at Gleason's, the performers in the big leagues, and the fans don't simply defend their sport. Rather everyone who is in on the game actively works to promote his or her definition of "real" wrestling. As I was nearing the end of my research at Gleason's, I sat for a while at ringside with Mohammed (23 July 1994). We watched Rubio and Frankie work out in silence for a while. I was admiring their acrobatics, the balletic grace with which they performed their exchanges, when Mohammed interrupted my rev-

Mohammed in pain, or is he?

erie to tell me why he doesn't like Lucha Libre. "It's too fake," he judged. I asked him if by fake he means that it's too visibly choreographed for his taste. He answered yes and continued: "American wrestling is more violent and aggressive. It's more real." Taking a breather, Rubio and Frankie then came to sit with us. Rubio, still perched on the apron of the ring, motioned to me, inviting me in: "Come on. Come wrestle with me. I'll let you throw me. You can be the tough guy. Promise." I declined and a month later moved to New Zealand.

Postscript

O n my penultimate visit to Gleason's Gym (16 July 1994) before
moving to New Zealand, Larry asked me if I considered myself a
fan. Genuinely stumped, I thought for a minute before responding
that I was no longer sure, but I didn't really think so. After another
silence, he said that he didn't think he was either. At least, we agreed,
we knew that most of the time we were not, although at moments we had
to admit to being as much marks as anyone else. Now, having written
this book, I would answer the question differently. Yes, of course I am a
fan. How could I have spent years in and out of the gym, attending
performances and collecting materials as well as conversations, if I were
not, on some level, as deeply engaged as the most hard-core fan? While
there have been many times in the researching when I, like the fans,
have wanted to stand up, chant "Bor-ring" and wait for the action to
pick up, I also have experienced moments of genuine exhilaration, both

during workouts and at performances. Like the hard-core fans and the wrestlers themselves, I have been rewarded for my patient presence with instances of breathtaking flight, incidents of fierce fighting, genuine intimacies, and a sense of community that I might not have otherwise experienced.

The Unpredictable School of Professional Wrestling is thriving these days, having received a tremendous push when Johnny Rodz was inducted into the World Wrestling Federation Hall of Fame in 1996. Many of the wrestlers who appear in this narrative have moved on. Indeed, by the time I left New York, Sky Magic had disappeared; although I am told she's moved on to boxing, I still imagine her touring Germany in her girl wrestler spectacle. But Chris and Vito are still regulars at Gleason's. Vito, I am told, has just returned from a ten-month tour of Puerto Rico. Larry Brisco still wrestles, still pursues the elusive dream of a major run in the big leagues, while as Laurence A. W. DeGaris he is now finishing his doctorate in sports sociology and writing about wrestling. When Larry and I reconnect via the Internet to discuss my book and his writing, he passes along the regards of the others. I am astonished by my nostalgia for those hot and dangerous days, and I am touched once again by their generosity in allowing me inside, at least for a time.

Notes

1. "The Doggie Doggie World of Professional Wrestling," *Drama Review* 34, no. 4 (T128) (Winter 1990); this original essay serves as the foundation stone for, and much of it has been integrated into, this book. Also: "In Search of the 'Morality' in Professional Wrestling's All-American Play" (conference paper, Association for Theatre in Higher Education/American Theatre and Drama Society, Chicago, 1990) and "From Beefcake to Cheesecake: The Appearance of Women in Professional Wrestling" (conference paper, Association for Theatre in Higher Education/Women and Theatre Program, Seattle, 1991). Parts of this chapter have been excerpted from an essay entitled "Watching Wrestling/Writing Performance" in *Hop on Pop: The Politics and Pleasures of Popular Culture* (Durham, N.C.: Duke University Press, forthcoming), which in turn was drawn from a conference paper (Association for Theatre in Higher Education/Performance Studies, San Francisco, 1995).

2. For discussions of wrestling's theatricality, see Morton and O'Brien. Also: "William E. Coleman Jr., "Where the Action Isn't: Toward a Rhetoric of Illusion," and Gerald Craven and Richard Moseley, "Actors on the Canvas Stage: The Dramatic Conventions of Professional Wrestling." Professional wrestling's theatricality is also exploited in a recent novel, *The Wrestler's Cruel Study,* by Stephen Dobyns, who imagines the wrestling world as a setting for his postmodern romp from the distance of the stands rather than from actual experience in the ring. For readings based in the idea of the folk, see the 1970s series of articles on wrestling's ritual aspects by Mark E. Workman as well as the more recent *Professional Wrestling as Ritual Drama in American Popular Culture* by Michael R. Ball.

3. In addition to the studies cited above, there are several focused specifically on wrestling's moral structure, for example: Erving Goffman, who in *Frame Analysis* uses his impressions of televised wrestling as paradigmatic of performances that consistently establish brackets in order that they may be transgressed (416–18), and Thomas Henricks in "Professional Wrestling as Moral Order."

4. Most studies of professional wrestling address its deployment of racial and national stereotypes, at least indirectly. For a direct consideration of these issues, see Brendan Maguire and John F. Wozniak, "Racial and Ethnic Stereotypes in Professional Wrestling."

CHAPTER 2. WHAT THE *WORLD* IS WATCHING

1. These figures were given to me as estimates by Steve Planamenta of the World Wrestling Federation in a telephone conversation (20 April 1989). As the WWF is privately owned, its records are not available to the public.

2. Indeed, the medievals were given to staging combat as a moral play. See Steven I. Pederson's discussion of the intersection between the joust and the moral interlude in *The Tournament Tradition and Staging "The Castle of Perseverance."*

3. See, for example, their discussion of wrestling's heroes and villains, pp. 129–30.

4. See also Morton and O'Brien, p. 66.

5. See also Henricks, pp. 184–86.

6. See also Coleman, p. 282.

CHAPTER 3. LEARNING THE GAME

1. From "RELEASE AND DISCHARGE," a contract absolving the school and Johnny of responsibility for injuries related directly or indirectly to training, which Johnny has all new trainees sign.

2. See Richard Schechner, *Between Theater and Anthropology*, p. 23.

3. Prominent in the list of professional wrestlers who began as amateurs are such stars as the Iron Sheik, Bob Backlund, General Adnan, the Steiner Brothers, and Owen Hart. See "Editorial: Amateurs Turn Pro" (in the August 1991 *Wrestling Eye*).

4. While I come up empty-handed during a moderately intensive search for the article Chris cites, I find a similar article in *Wrestling Today* from about the same time, and it is possible that he has misremembered in this case.

5. As with other aspects of professional wrestling, concrete information in this regard is almost impossible to come by without paying the fee oneself.

CHAPTER 4. REAL MEN DON'T WEAR SHIRTS

1. *Wrestling's Greatest Villains: The Golden Era. Exciting Highlights from '50s & '60s TV.* Goodtimes Home Video, 1986.

2. *Wrestling's Greatest Heroes: The Golden Era: Exciting Highlights from '50s and '60s TV.* Goodtimes Home Video, 1986.

3. In his book *Masculinity and Power,* Arthur Brittan notes: "Masculinity from this point of view [social Darwinism] is measured by a man's capacity to win" (79).

4. Don Sabo in *Sex, Violence and Power in Sports* tells us that for boys who are becoming men "to endure pain is courageous, to survive pain is manly" (86). In Brian Pronger's words: "The pain is worth it, because masculinity is worth it" (23).

5. Brittan declares, "We cannot talk of masculinity, only masculinities" (1), and he later adds: "Masculinity is a relational construct. It only exists in relation to femininity" (195). Michael Messner, in *Power at Play: Sports and the Problem of Masculinity,* is even more to the point when he notes: "Sport is a domain of contested national, class, and racial relations, but the hegemonic conception of masculinity in sport also bonds men, at least symbolically, as a separate and superior group to women" (19). In another essay, he clarifies his polemic: "Violent sports as spectacle provide linkages among men in the project of the domination of women while at the same time helping to construct and clarify differences among various masculinities" ("Masculinities and Athletic Careers" 103).

6. Throughout his study of homosexuality in sports, *The Arena of Masculinity,* Brian Pronger attempts to wrench wrestling—both amateur and professional—along with other contact sports out of the closet, at one point noting that there is a thriving industry in explicitly homoerotic wrestling video production and distribution (183). Moreover, I was told in an informal conversation in 1991 by Martin Worman that there are weekly wrestling events in the gay community in Greenwich Village that are simultaneously closer to amateur practice and more explicitly erotic than professional wrestling.

7. Messner points to the tension between homophobia and homosexuality in sport as a whole: "In short, competitive activities such as sport mediate men's relationships with each other in ways that allow them to develop a powerful bond while at the same time preventing the development of intimacy" (*Power at Play* 91).

CHAPTER 5. FROM BEEFCAKE TO CHEESECAKE

1. Misty Blue and Linda Dallas have worked together frequently to pro-duce pornographic wrestling videos, in which they star, with Misty's hus-band doing double duty as referee and photographer. At least one of their videos has been circulated among the wrestlers at Gleason's (Larry DeGaris, e-mail correspondence 24 December 1996 and 3 January 1997).

2. Re: Hatpin Mary, see Chad Dell, pp. 94–95. For an extended descrip-tion of an elderly female fan known as Ma Pickles, see Jim Freedman, pp. 23–31.

3. In a rather ironic coda to the public (re)staging of their wedding vows, the two were divorced the subsequent year (1992).

4. The staging of weddings is historically a common way of generating heat in popular performance, a practice that extends well beyond wrestling to the sideshow, marathon dancing, and off-Broadway productions. See, for example, accounts in Leslie Fiedler's *Freaks: Myths and Images of the Secret Self* (New York: Simon and Schuster, 1978) and in Carol Martin's *Dance Marathons: Performing American Culture in the 1920s and 1930s* (Jackson: Uni-versity Press of Mississippi, 1994), as well as the long-running hit show *Tony and Tina's Wedding* (New York City).

5. *The Best of Women's Championship Wrestling*, volume 1 (Video Gems).

6. *GLOW: Gorgeous Ladies of Wrestling* (Today Home Entertainment; David McLane Enterprises).

CHAPTER 6. "REAL" LIFE

1. This incident is discussed from the fanzine perspective in "The Rene-gades of the Ring" (*Wrestling World*) by Jerry Prater, who explains: "Ali is a superb athlete, a former Olympic competitor and coach; but having once been a bodyguard for the Shah of Iran, he isn't too anxious to get deported back to his home country for punching out a reporter." And he adds: "I have personally seen the Iron Sheik dispose of several irate, chair-wielding fans who went after him outside the ring, so there can hardly be any doubt as to the damge [sic] he could inflict on one wise-cracking reporter" (35–36).

2. A parenthetical comment under the heading "It's Only Wrestling, Right?" in "News & Analysis" of the World Wrestling Federation. *Pro Wres-tling Torch* 207 (28 December 1992), p. 2.

3. MacNeeley was Tyson's first postprison opponent and lost as a result of a rather preemptive disqualification.

4. My videotape of this sequence was unaccountably erased, so the date of the episode (as well as its replays) is unavailable.

Sources

PRIMARY SOURCES

Interviews, Conversations, Encounters

Albano, "Captain" Lou. Telephone interview with author, 18 July 1989.

Anonymous woman. Conversation with author, Gleason's Arena, Brooklyn, N.Y., 2 October 1993.

Brisco, Larry (Laurence A. W. DeGaris). Conversation with author, Gleason's Arena, Brooklyn, N.Y., 11 April 1989.

———. Conversation with author, Gleason's Gym, Brooklyn, N.Y., 20 February 1993.

———. Conversation with author, Gleason's Gym, Brooklyn, N.Y., 17 April 1993.

———. Conversation with author, Gleason's Gym, Brooklyn, N.Y., 5 May 1993.

———. Conversation with author, Gleason's Gym, Brooklyn, N.Y., 17 July 1993.

———. Conversation with author, Gleason's Gym, Brooklyn, N.Y., 25 June 1994.

———. Conversation with author, Gleason's Gym, Brooklyn, N.Y., 16 July 1994.

———. E-mail correspondence with author, 23 December 1996.

———. E-mail correspondence with author, 24 December 1996.

———. E-mail correspondence with author, 3 January 1997.

———. E-mail correspondence with author, 24 January 1997.

———. E-mail correspondence with author, 26 January 1997.

———. E-mail correspondence with author, 27 January 1997.

Deak, Julius. Conversation with author, Gleason's Arena, Brooklyn, N.Y., 18 August 1989.

DeVito, Steve. Conversation with author, Gleason's Arena, Brooklyn, N.Y., 11 April 1989.

Frankie. Conversation with author, Gleason's Gym, Brooklyn, N.Y., 25 September 1993.

Lagerstrom, Benjamin (a.k.a. Big Daddy Money Bucks and the Shoeshine Boy). Conversation with author, Joe Bar, New York City, 2 August 1994.

Little White Wolf (Adolfo). Conversation with author, Gleason's Arena, Brooklyn, N.Y., 11 April 1989.

Mikulewicz, Bil. Conversation with author, New York City, 5 March 1993.

Moniz, Chris. Conversation with author, Barnes and Noble Café, New York City, 5 August 1994.

Nazim, Mohammed (Indio). Conversation with author, Gleason's Gym, Brooklyn, N.Y., 5 May 1993.

———. Conversation with author, Gleason's Gym, Brooklyn, N.Y., 23 July 1994.

Planamenta, Steve. Telephone interview with author, 20 April 1989.

Rodz, Johnny. Conversation with author, Gleason's Arena, Brooklyn, N.Y., 10, 11, 18, 21 April 1989.

———. Telephone interview with author, 20 November 1989.

———. Conversation with author, Gleason's Gym, Brooklyn, N.Y., 30 January 1993.

———. Conversation with author, in the car from Brooklyn to New York City, 9 February 1993.

———. Conversation with author, Gleason's Gym, Brooklyn, N.Y., 19 May 1993.

Rubio. Conversation with author, Gleason's Gym, Brooklyn, N.Y., 31 July 1993.

———. Conversation with author, Gleason's Gym, Brooklyn, N.Y., 21 August 1993.

———. Conversation with author, Gleason's Gym, Brooklyn, N.Y., 25 September 1993.

Sky Magic. Conversation with author, Gleason's Gym, Brooklyn, N.Y., 5 May 1993.

———. Conversation with author, Gleason's Gym, Brooklyn, N.Y., 31 July 1993.

———. Conversations with author, Gleason's Gym, Brooklyn, N.Y., and the F Train, 2 August 1993.

———. Conversation with author, Gleason's Gym, Brooklyn, N.Y., 25 September 1993.

————. Conversation with author, Gleason's Gym, Brooklyn, NY, 2 October 1993.

Sonntag, Katy. E-mail correspondence with author, 9 December 1996.

Tony. Conversation with author, Gleason's Gym, Brooklyn, N.Y., 25 September 1993.

Vito. Encounter with author, Gleason's Gym, Brooklyn, N.Y., 20 February 1993.

————. Conversation with author, Gleason's Gym, Brooklyn, N.Y., 29 February 1993.

————. Conversation with author, Gleason's Gym, Brooklyn, N.Y., 21 August 1993.

Magazines and Journals

"CATFIGHT Special!" Advertisement in *Wrestling Eye,* August 1991, p. 11.

Feintuch, Howard. "Wrestling Schools: First Step to Becoming a Pro Wrestler." *Wrestling Today* 1, no. 25 (1991 Annual), p. 90–94.

"The Fierce World of Female Fighting." Advertisement in *Wrestling's Main Event,* September 1991, p. 51.

"FIGHTING FEMMES." Advertisement in *Wrestling Eye,* August 1991, p. 10.

"Grab the Scoop!" Advertisement in *Wrestling World,* March 1990, p. 7.

"HUMILIATION." Advertisement in *Wrestling Eye,* August 1991, p. 53.

Krebs, Sandy. "Hello Miss Elizabeth! Goodbye Macho King??" *Wrestling's Main Event,* September 1991, pp. 28–30.

"The Live Wrestling Slam Line." Advertisement in *Wrestling Eye,* August 1991, back cover.

Marx, Hubie. "Editorial: Amateurs Turn Pro." *Wrestling Eye,* August 1991, p. 5.

"News & Analysis" (of the World Wrestling Federation). *Pro Wrestling Torch,* 28 December 1992.

Prater, Jerry. "Renegades of the Ring." *Wrestling World,* March 1990, pp. 32–36.

"ROCK HARD STRONG AND SEXY." Advertisement in back pages of the *Village Voice,* 5 July 1994.

"SLIPPERY WHEN WET." Advertisement in *Wrestling Eye,* June 1993, p. 7.

Pamphlets and Other Materials

New York State Athletic Commission. *Laws and Rules Regulating Boxing and Wrestling Matches.* 1984.

————. *Special Rules for Wrestling.* 1984.

Rodz, Johnny. "RELEASE AND DISCHARGE." Contract with the Unpredictable School of Professional Wrestling Training Center, Brooklyn, N.Y. n.d.

RSPW: Rec.sport.pro-wrestling (Internet Discussion Group)

Carrington, Mattie (carringt@sonoma.edu). "Re: [WCW] Would you like a Frosty Beverage, Mr. Bischoff?" 12 December 1996.

———. "Re: WWF vs. WCW vs. ECW vs. Stampede Wrestling." 12 December 1996.

———. "Re: WWF vs. WCW vs. ECW vs. Stampede Wrestling." 13 December 1996.

Chung, Richard K. (no e-mail address). "Re: Micheals [sic] collapse last year, work or shoot?" 20 December 1996.

Councell (councell@erols.com). "Re: What if Vince had thought up the NWO." 6 January 1997.

Gokhale, Milan (mira-g@netcom.ca). "Re: Micheals [sic] collapse last year, work or shoot?" 22 December 1996.

Grant, Ryan (RCGrant@earthlink.net). "Re: [Raw] Bret a Republican?" 3 January 1997.

Haller, Timothy (afa53940@afa.org). "Re: [Raw] Bret a Republican?" 3 January 1997.

Horowitz, Charles Eric (ceh1@acpub.duke.edu). "Re: What was the fan thinking?!?!" 30 December 1996.

Long, David (see.my.sig@bottom.for.email). "Re: What was the fan thinking?!?!" 30 December 1996.

Malecki, Mike (no e-mail address). "Re: Update on Billy's Condition?" 18 December 1996.

Meisner, Timothy (meisner@u.washington.edu). "Re: Micheals [sic] collapse last year, work or shoot?" 20 December 1996.

Mirza, Mustafa (makmirza@chat.carlton.edu). "Michaels/Bret angle—I'm confused." 6 January 1997.

Powerhug (powrhug@sky.net). "Re: "Micheals [sic] collapse last year, work or shoot?" 22 December 1996.

Sheir, Richard (rsheir@freenet.columbus.oh.us). "(RIP) Harry Helmsley Dead at 87." 6 January 1997.

Slugger 123 (slugger123@geocities.com). "Re: Billy Gunn Injury." 18 December 1996.

Stone Cold Paul Smith (Psmith80@concentric.net). "Re: [Raw] Bret a Republican?" 31 December 1996.

The Superfans (superfan@redrose.net). "Re: Who has better Pay-Per-Views—WWF or WCW? It's a no brainer!" 1 January 1997.

Thompson, Joseph (coot@walker0–194.reshall.on.edu). "Re: Update on Billy's condition?" 18 December 1996.

Unsigned (bobmcc@insync.net). No date. As quoted by Chris Ariens (ariens @globalserve.net). "Re: WHY DO PEOPLE BELIEVE I FAKE FIGHTING?" 19 December 1996.

Unsigned (interneg@aol.com). "Bishoff [sic] the Bore." 31 December 1996.

Unsigned (stevk@usit.net). "Re: What was the fan thinking?!?!" 1 January 1997.

Unsigned (sza 500@teleweb.net). "Re: [Raw] Bret a Republican?" 3 January 1997.

Television Broadcasts and Videos

20/20. ABC-TV. 21 February 1985.

The Best of Women's Championship Wrestling, volume 1. Video Gems.

GLOW: Gorgeous Ladies of Wrestling. Today Home Entertainment; David McLane Enterprises.

I Remember Gorgeous George. PBS Special, produced and directed by Clifton Jolley. n.d.

WCW Pro Wrestling. 22 June 1991.

WCW Pro Wrestling. 6 July 1991.

WrestleMania V. 2 April 1989.

WrestleMania IX. 4 April 1993.

WrestleMania X. 20 March 1994.

Wrestling's Greatest Heroes: The Golden Era: Exciting Highlights from '50s and '60s TV. Goodtimes Home Video, 1986.

Wrestling's Greatest Villains: The Golden Era: Exciting Highlights from '50s and '60s TV. Goodtimes Home Video, 1986.

WWF Superstars of Wrestling. 22 April 1989.

WWF Superstars of Wrestling. 1 July 1989.

WWF Wrestling Challenge. 27 August 1989.

WWF Wrestling Spotlight. 6 July 1991.

SECONDARY SOURCES

Articles and Essays

Barthes, Roland. "The World of Wrestling." In *Mythologies.* Selected and translated from the French by Annette Lavers. 1957. Reprint, New York: Hill and Wang, 1972.

Carter, Angela. "Giant's Playtime." *New Society* 29 (January 1976): 227–28.

Coleman, William E., Jr. "Where the Action Isn't: Toward a Rhetoric of Illusion." *Et Cetera* (Fall 1989): 276–85.

Craven, Gerald, and Richard Moseley. "Actors on the Canvas Stage: The Dramatic Conventions of Professional Wrestling." *Journal of Popular Culture* 6, no. 2 (Fall 1972): 325–36.

DeGaris, Laurence A. W. "Professional Wrestling's Commercial Exploitation of Homophobia." Paper presented at the annual NASSS Conference in Birmingham, Ala., 1996.

Dell, Chad. " 'Lookit That Hunk of Man!': Subversive Pleasures, Female Fandom and Professional Wrestling." *Theorizing Fandom: Fans, Subculture, and Identity.* Edited by Cheryl Harris and Alison Alexander. Cresskill, N.J.: Hampton Press, forthcoming.

Fussell, Sam. "Bodybuilder Americanus." In *The Male Body: Features, Destinies, Exposures.* Ann Arbor: University of Michigan Press, 1994.

"Gold Fuss." *New York Times Magazine,* 22 September 1996, p. 21.

Gutowski, John A. "The Art of Professional Wrestling: Folk Expression in Mass Culture." *Keystone Folklore Quarterly* 17, no. 2 (Summer 1972): 41–50.

Henricks, Thomas. "Professional Wrestling as Moral Order." *Sociological Inquiry* 44, no. 3 (1974): 177–88.

Jenkins, Henry, III. " 'Never Trust a Snake': WWF Wrestling as Masculine Melodrama." Unpublished paper, 1992.

Kerrick, G. E. "The Jargon of Professional Wrestling." *American Speech* 55 (1980): 142–45.

Maguire, Brendan, and John F. Wozniak. "Racial and Ethnic Stereotypes in Professional Wrestling." *Social Science Journal* 24, no. 3 (1987): 261–73.

Martin, William C. "Friday Night in the Coliseum." *Atlantic* 29 (March 1972): 83–87.

Messner, Michael A. "Masculinities and Athletic Careers: Bonding and Status Differences." In *Sport, Men and the Gender Order: Critical Feminist Perspectives.* Edited by Michael A. Messner and Donald F. Sabo. Champaign, Ill.: Human Kinetics, 1990.

Sorkin, Michael. "Simulations: Faking It." In *Watching Television: A Pantheon Guide to Popular Culture.* Edited by Todd Gitlin. New York: Pantheon, 1986.

Workman, Mark E. "The Differential Perception of Popular Dramatic Events." *Keystone Folklore Quarterly* 23, no. 3 (Summer 1979): 1–10.

———. "Dramaturgical Aspects of Professional Wrestling." *Folklore Forum* 10 (1977): 14–20.

———. "Structural and Symbolic Aspects of a Contemporary Ritual Event." *Keystone Folklore Quarterly* 20, no. 3 (Summer 1975): 19–31.

Books

Aristotle. *Poetics.* Translated by S. H. Butcher. Introduction by Francis Fergusson. 1961. Reprint, New York: Hill and Wang, 1984.

Artaud, Atonin. *The Theatre and its Double.* Translated by Mary Caroline Richards. New York: Grove Press, 1958.

Bakhtin, M. M. *The Dialogic Imagination: Four Essays.* Edited by Michael Holquist. Translated by Caryl Emerson and Michael Holquist. Austin: University of Texas Press, 1981.

————. *Rabelais and His World.* Translated by Hélène Iswolsky. 1968. Reprint, Bloomington: Indiana University Press, 1984.

Ball, Michael R. *Professional Wrestling as Ritual Drama in American Popular Culture.* Mellen Studies in Sociology, volume 8. Lewiston, N.Y.: Edwin Mellen Press, 1990.

Baudrillard, Jean. *Simulations.* Translated by Paul Foss, Paul Patton, and Philip Beitchman. New York: Semiotext(e), 1983.

Bly, Robert. *Iron John: A Book About Men.* Reading, Mass.: Addison-Wesley, 1990.

Brittan, Arthur. *Masculinity and Power.* New York and Oxford: Basil Blackwell, 1989.

Dobyns, Stephen. *The Wrestler's Cruel Study.* New York and London: Norton, 1993.

Dutton, Kenneth R. *The Perfectible Body: The Western Ideal of Physical Development.* London: Cassell, 1995.

Eco, Umberto. *Travels in Hyperreality.* Translated by William Weaver. 1967. Reprint, Orlando, Fla.: Harcourt, Brace, Jovanovich, 1986.

Fiedler, Leslie. *Freaks: Myths and Images of the Secret Self.* New York: Simon and Schuster, 1978.

Freedman, Jim. *Drawing Heat.* Ontario: Black Moss, 1988.

Geertz, Clifford. *The Interpretation of Cultures.* New York: Basic Books, 1973.

Guttman, Allen. *Sports Spectators.* New York: Columbia University Press, 1986.

Jarman, Tom, and Reid Hanley. *Wrestling for Beginners.* Chicago: Contemporary Books, 1983.

Jenkins, Henry. *Textual Poachers: Television Fans and Participatory Culture.* New York and London: Routledge, 1992.

Lehman, Peter. *Running Scared: Masculinity and the Representation of the Male Body.* Philadelphia: Temple University Press, 1993.

Martin, Carol. *Dance Marathons: Performing American Culture in the 1920s and 1930s.* Jackson, Miss.: University Press of Mississippi, 1994.

Messner, Michael A. *Power at Play: Sports and the Problem of Masculinity.* Boston: Beacon Press, 1992.

Messner, Michael A., and Donald F. Sabo. *Sex, Violence, and Power in Sports: Rethinking Masculinity.* Freedom, Calif.: Crossing Press, 1994.

Meyer, Moe, ed. *The Politics and Poetics of Camp.* London and New York: Routledge, 1994.

Morgan, Roberta. *Main Event: The World of Professional Wrestling.* New York: Dial Press, 1979.

Morton, Gerald W., and George M. O'Brien. *Wrestling to Rasslin: Ancient Sport to American Spectacle.* Bowling Green, Ohio: Bowling Green State University Popular Press, 1985.

Pederson, Steven I. *The Tournament Tradition and Staging "The Castle of Perseverance."* 1983. Reprint, Ann Arbor, Mich.: UMI Research Press, 1987.

Pronger, Brian. *The Arena of Masculinity: Sports, Homosexuality, and the Meaning of Sex.* New York: St. Martin's Press, 1990.

Sansome, David. *Greek Athletics and the Genesis of Sport.* Berkeley and Los Angeles: University of California Press, 1988.

Schechner, Richard. *Between Theater and Anthropology.* Foreword by Victor Turner. Philadelphia: University of Pennsylvania Press, 1985.

Senelick, Lawrence, ed. *Gender in Performance: The Presentation of Difference in the Performing Arts.* Hanover, N.H., and London: University Press of New England, 1992.

Turner, Victor. *From Ritual to Theatre: The Human Seriousness of Play.* New York: PAJ Publications, 1982.

Twitchell, James B. *Carnival Culture: The Trashing of Taste in America.* New York: Columbia University Press, 1992.

———. *Preposterous Violence: Fables of Aggression in Modern Culture.* New York and Oxford: Oxford University Press, 1989.

Index